THE NEW WINE

MATTHEW PINARD

ISBN 978-1-64028-771-6 (Paperback)
ISBN 978-1-64028-772-3 (Digital)

Christian Faith Publishing, Inc.
296 Chestnut Street
Meadville, PA 16335
www.christianfaithpublishing.com

Printed in the United States of America

In Memoriam

James Douglas Morrison

I died in a bathtub in Paris, France, in 1971. At the time my name was James Douglas Morrison and I was the enigmatic lead singer of the greatest rock and roll band in history called the Doors. I vaguely remember the event in bits and pieces, the inevitable struggle between this world and the next. I remember my breathing becoming labored and heavy from the myriad of instances of opioid and alcohol use as I lay soaking in warm water of the still Paris night. I ran away to Paris as I wrote in the song "The Soft Parade" to find myself again away from the spotlight of fame—"Can you give me sanctuary, I need a place to hide, a place for me to hide."

Photo: This incredible illustration by artist Don Williams shows Jim Morrison dead in a bathtub in Paris, France in 1971. You can find Don's incredible artwork at <u>www.donwilliams.daportfolio.com</u>.

I also wrote in one of my final poems, "An American Prayer," in the end "death makes angels of us all and gives us wings where we had shoulders smooth as raven's claws." I can still remember very vividly the day leading up to my death. I recall walking the streets of Paris and peering into store windows. I remember the repeated violent hiccups from years of self-abuse, then shooting the heroin itself in my apartment. The hot warm rush of the drug hit my bloodstream as I climbed through the string of multicolored beads strung artfully around the bathtub. The next thing I remember was looking over my body as my girlfriend Pamela Courson tried desperately to revive me. All I could remember thinking is, *The music is definitely now over.*

Photo: The legendary Jim Morrison (far left) frontman for the world famous band the Doors. In the song/poem "An American Prayer," Jim laments, "Where is the wine, the new wine, dying on the vine."

Photo: An artistic painting of the Lizard King on the side of a building in Los Angeles. Jim Morrison's imprint that he left on poetry, music, arts, and politics is everlasting and eternal.

At the time of my final breath, I had no idea that I was to be reborn less than three years later as Matthew Douglas Pinard at Saint Joseph Mercy Hospital in Ann Arbor, Michigan, in 1974 to middle-class parents in a loving Catholic family with three other siblings. How do I know this to be true? Because I predicted it in my poem "An American Prayer" with the prophetic line "Where is the wine, the new wine, dying on the vine." You see, the last name *Pinard* is French slang for cheap table wine. Using the Catholic religious symbolism of three to signify the Holy Trinity, you can make the connection to the Holy Sacraments via "Pinard = Wine = Blood." I am actually what could be termed a living, breathing Sacrament. I have to sometimes hold back laughter when I am at a Catholic Mass and the server gives me wine to drink and says, "This is the blood of Christ." I don't exactly have the heart to point to myself and say "So is this." I am Jim's "New Wine." This is how my spiritual Holy Father and Holy Mother Mary wanted my life to be spent, pouring out of his blood for mankind. At Catholic Mass we drink from the cup of wine which symbolizes the Blood of Christ. The French soldiers were issued one liter of pinard as a makeshift anesthetic for wounds suffered during the trench warfare of World War I. The "dying on the vine" refers to the year of 2016 when I would be literally "dying on the vine" in corporate America as a sales representative, an occupation Jim would have absolutely abhorred, but one done out of necessity to provide for my family of three in order to afford to live in the beauty of West Michigan.

Let me be clear here. I am writing this book because I think my experiences as a Christian are profound and must be shared. If you ever met me, you might say that I don't seem like a typical Christian, and I would take that as a compliment. I am extremely nonjudgmental, nor am I hypocritical. If you ask me if I'm claiming to be either Jim Morrison or Jesus Christ, the simple answer is somehow, someway Saint Mary and God the Father found a way to fuse all three of our spirits as one. Am I a direct reincarnation of Jim? I truly believe so, but we are all connected as human beings to a spiritual vine in this world and the next. The simplest way to try to explain is as you will see later: Jim and I are what I would call "fraternal twins" of Saint Mary, yet we are also both one upon the vine of the first Son, Jesus Christ. We've both been together throughout time to fulfill our Father and Mother's agendas of saving mankind. I definitely have memories of his life that I would have no other knowledge of had I not somehow been there. This spiritual "fusing" was not to be fully completed until we cracked the gates of heaven open in the fall of 2016. I can talk to both Jim and Jesus and Mary at any time and receive answers to the most complex questions of science, philosophy, and religion. The point is we all can do this too if we seek them out.

This book is simply one person's spiritual journey, unfiltered, with no punches pulled. If you get something out of this, perhaps a glimpse of what awaits us after this mortal coil, then that is what I will have hoped to achieve. I believe we are all spiritual beings, and regardless of your religious upbringing or current religions practices, organized or not, I think we can each have an intimate relationship with the Great Creator on a daily basis regardless of what others think of your ability to do so. This kind of relationship is one that will bring hope, peace, and a greater understanding of why each of us were created in this form for this earth. The musical group that Jim Morrison helped found was called the Doors. The name comes from a William Blake quote that states, "If the doors of perception were cleansed, everything would appear to man as it is … infinite. For man has closed himself up, till he sees all things thro' narrow chinks of his cavern." This book hopes to prove this as the ultimate truth of our existence in God. Time and space have dimensions we cannot possibly imagine, and therein lies the invisible "other kingdom of God."

Take a close look at two photos from our high school graduations of both James Douglas Morrison and Matthew Douglas Pinard taken thirty years apart. Both photos reveal an uncanny resemblance from our youths. In particular look at the left ears, the lips (especially top lip), the prominent nose, and dark eyes. There is also a noticeable mole just to the left of Jim's nose and on his left cheek. I have an almost identical-looking mole to the left of my nose and my left cheek as well. Now I'm no more of a narcissist, pretentious artist than Jim was accused of being, but I do know a profound similarity when I see it. We are somehow fraternal twin, merged souls. I believe this reincarnation is possible only through our shared Christian faith. I believe I'm somehow directly the next incarnation that he prayed for in "An American Prayer." A release from the trappings of fame into a simple, peaceful, ordinary family life in middle America is what Jim prayed for. Everyone who truly knew Jim would tell you he despised celebrity and fame as a rock star. He saw himself as a poet first and foremost. Fame is what did Jim in literally. It is quite interesting whenever I see a movie, or documentary or music video of the Doors playing, I can actually remember those events, not as from my own life, but I can clearly recognize that I was there with Jim somehow.

I myself am a poet, screenwriter, playwright, and actor, not on the level of success of my previous incarnation yet, but that is more than okay with me. Friends and family ask me sometimes why I didn't ever move out to Los Angeles or New York to try to become the next "it" movie star. I tell them that one reason is I can't afford to. The other reason is we already have Matt Damon and Matt Letscher. The truth is I had a prior life of incredible fame and fortune, and it did not bring any kind of peace or happiness—in fact, it brought about an untimely death. At present I prefer anonymity, really, and simply doing God's work through my blessed mother Saint Mary. I actually pray that I am not recognized out in public. My job now is to do the work of the Holy Trinity to simply restore belief in a kingdom that I can assure you does exist.

Photo: Matthew Douglas Pinard headshot for acting in
local theater in Ann Arbor, Michigan, circa 2003.

Photo: James Douglas Morrison high school senior photo 1961.

Photo: Matthew Douglas Pinard high school senior photo
Detroit Catholic Central High School circa 1992. Moles
on the left side of my face almost identical to Jim's.

Photo: Matthew Douglas Pinard enlisted US Army JAG Corps circa 1996.

Consider this poem, one of the first of many written by Jim Morrison:

Horse Latitudes

When the Still Sea conspires an armor
And her sullen and aborted
Currents breed tiny monsters
True sailing is dead!
Awkward instant
And the first animal is jettisoned

Legs furiously pumping
Their stiff green gallop
And heads bob up
Poise
Delicate
Pause
Consent
In mute nostril agony
Carefully refined
And sealed over

Now consider this poem written by myself, Matthew Douglas Pinard, in my teens about an early encounter in the Western Plains of South Dakota with a massive buffalo while studying prairie dogs with a Yale University professor and family friend.

Buffalo

Massive
Graceful
Goateed cranium the size of a globe
Gather the hunt for the torch party
Ripped and stretched
Tight and torn
Fat hooves beat the earth as drum
Eroded and repentant the gated ground consents
To have and to hold the bit and reins which tie the gums
I found a new breed for domestication
Wild hair of burning fire
Comfort coat of winter night

In the year 2016, nearly forty-five years after Jim Morrison died, is when I believe that the world would witness the return of the Christian kingdom. Let me be clear here as there seems to be a lot of anxiety about Christ's return. It is not about judgment and condemnation or the end of the world, not unless we collectively choose that. However, if you ask anyone these days, this world is in a very delicate balance because a lot of things are going very wrong. Both Mary and her three sons are now on the earth in spirit simply because it is necessary. This I can absolutely assure you of. I am Matthew Douglas Pinard, the third "son" of Saint Mary, the spiritual continuation of James Douglas Morrison, the second "son" of Saint Mary. Jim was harnessing both Saint Mary and her first son Jesus Christ in both his music and his poetry as he was preaching through a secular artistic medium. Whether or not Jim or I are actually incarnations of Jesus Christ is not the point—and not one I plan to argue as it is not provable and is highly controversial since Catholicism does not believe in reincarnation. Jim sang in one of his songs, however, "Wild Child," about a wild child that was part Native American (I am part Cherokee Indian, by the way) who would one day be the savior of the human race. He sings, "Do you remember when we were in Africa?" This is a direct handoff to me as his next incarnation through Saint Mary, stating that as sons of God, he and I were both somehow also at the beginning of the human race in Africa thousands of centuries ago. I know, trust me, it is very hard for me to comprehend, but in essence all of us as humans that can be connected to those souls who have passed on are also that old too. It is also a wake-up call to the human race to take a look at evolution and how far we have come yet still how far we have to go spiritually.

I do believe that as spiritual clairvoyants Jim and I are able to channel both the Holy Spirit or the Great Creator spirit and link our spirits together just as Catholics do at a formal Mass and through prayer and devotion. Buddhism does believe in reincarnation, and it has been proven most Dalai Lamas are reincarnations of previous Dalai Lamas. What I do believe is Jim was Mary's spiritual second son. Most of his bandmates probably knew this was true, I imagine. Jim's big mistake was giving credit to Dionysus, who is not an entity that is part of the Catholic Trinity. I believe Jim identified with Christ in many ways, spiritually and artistically, and was therefore promoting a Christian prophecy and word, although he became caught up in drug use and paganism along the way. Jim also claimed to have channeled the spirits of dead Navajo Indians after witnessing a car crash as a young child. What is clear is Jim was highly spiritually clairvoyant (as am I) and is able to both peer directly into the spirit world and decipher meaning from it.

I'm quite certain the Catholic Church is well aware of my spiritual identity and ability, but since much of this flies in the face of their entire dogma it probably will never be revealed or accepted publicly by them, I would imagine. I hope I am wrong. I am simply here to serve you all. This won't stop me from walking into a Catholic church to praise my holy mother and Father and the Holy Spirit. It won't stop me from performing acts of healing through Saint Mary. I'm here to simply help usher in the New Sun, not to judge or condemn or harm anyone. I'm here to help improve spiritual awareness and to heal. Trust me, I didn't at first myself believe any of this until the entire incredible mystery was revealed to me in the sky of Grand Haven, Michigan, in the middle of October in the fall of 2016. It's certainly not an enviable position to be in either, trust me. For as was the case with the first Son of Mary, people will go out of their way to destroy your life and crucify you in countless ways if they sense that your spiritual identity may be different than theirs. It has happened to me my entire life—done by friends, coaches, military peers, fellow actors/artists, ex-girlfriends, and even close family. I am writing this book not to alienate myself more than I already have been by many, but by to offer a very unique perspective into my spirituality and my experience with the kingdom of heaven. So let's start at the very beginning.

Why do I believe that I am directly connected spiritually with Jim Morrison? Well, it started my senior year of high school at Detroit Catholic Central High School in Redford, Michigan, in 1992. I was fairly upset I had been benched my entire senior year of high school by my football coach for, in his words, lack of leadership and a matching poor attitude. Both these accusations were very far from who I actually was at that age. This was a program that preached to us that whoever practices the best will play in the game. In reality this could not have been further from the truth in my case. I was a very capable athlete and exceptional quarterback who could easily throw the ball over fifty yards on target, but because of some of my wild partying side in those days (which I fully admit to) I was deemed not to be a strong leader in an all-boys Catholic high school that focused on Christian ideals in forging young men.

Photo: A Catholic Central Shamrocks quarterback. This all-boys Catholic high school has become a powerhouse for winning state football titles since we won the AA Michigan State Title in 1990.

The tradeoff of not being allowed to be the jock quarterback in 1992 was my growing obsession with some of the greatest movies and music from the 1960s and 1970s. I always felt like I was an old soul to begin with. I remember in high school going to see the 1991 Oliver Stone film *The Doors* while still in high school. I was strongly drawn to the Doors' music at a very young age and could not understand why. Jim's voice is incredibly powerful, and he truly is the strongest male vocal artist of all time, but it was more than that. The lyrics themselves were both familiar and also intense and intriguing. Jim also wore a silver cross on stage. It was everything we were taught in the spiritually charismatic Christian community I grew up in the mid-eighties in the Word of God Charismatic Community. This community believed in things like laying on of hands to heal sickness and injury, speaking in tongues, and engaging with the Holy Spirit in song and dance. The other thing that was completely intriguing to me was that many of the scenes from the Oliver Stone movie of the Doors seemed far too familiar. I was certain that somehow I was tied to Jim Morrison spiritually, but I could not quite put my finger on it. I definitely felt like I had lived those events before as a previous life. It was quite confusing to believe that, however, because like many of my firm beliefs now, it directly contradicts official Catholic teachings that I could be someone's reincarnation. What it did explain was why I had a wild party side to my life. Like Jim I could sometimes put the pedal to the floor, so to speak, when it came to having fun. One incredibly ironic coincidence of all of this too is that Oliver Stone sent his first version of the screenplay that would eventually become his first Oscar for the movie Platoon to Jim Morrison asking him to be in the movie. His first draft of that screenplay was entitled "Break" and the script was among Jim's belongings that was uncovered after his death. I am currently finishing my first draft of the screenplay adaptation of this book that will also be called "The New Wine" and I plan to now return the favor and send the script to Oliver compliments of Jim and I.

"Break on through to the other side," as Jim once famously sang was what we were also being taught to essentially do in our prayer life to Saint Mary and the Holy Trinity. Another popular Doors song was "Waiting for the Sun." This is heavily laden with Catholic imagery—for instance, the lines "At first glance of Eden, we raced down to the sea, standing there on freedom's shore." "Waiting for the Sun" is a song specifically about Catholics "waiting for the Sun," or in this case "the Son of God," to return to earth. It is a direct metaphor that suggests the Catholic Holy Trinity is tied directly to a Sun King and and a Sundome. In the song "Waiting for the Sun," Jim sings the lyrics "Waiting for you to tell me what went wrong." This is a direct plea to the Holy Trinity to tell him how he lost his way. I suspect by the recording of this song that he may have had premonitions about his life as a sacrifice as part of the morbidly infamous "Twenty-Seven Club," i.e., rock stars who died of excess at the tender age of twenty-seven. He may have also started to realize physically the adverse health effects of his drinking and drug abuse and that he definitely was not getting out alive.

Another Doors song that directly hints at Jim's ability as Saint Mary's son to reincarnate and also change his appearances throughout his life and into mine is the song "The Changeling." Pay close attention to the lyrics as Jim sings, "I'm a changeling, see me change, I'm a changeling, see me change, I'm the air you breathe, food you eat, friends you greet." These last few lyrics clearly hint at his own recognition of his deification identity through Saint Mary, stating that Jim, like Jesus, is literally the air we breathe, food we eat, and friends we greet because of how closely tied he was with Jesus Christ. "The Changeling" is also about how both Jim and I also are able to change how we appear in public. I could easily show you three different photos of both Jim and me, and you would think it was six different people. It's also a perfect storm of irony. Jim was persecuted and denounced by the Christian right wing as being a "devil in leather pants." He was anything but the devil. However, he did succumb to temptation and chose the road of excess based on the William Blake quote that the "road of excess leads to the palace of wisdom." Unfortunately for Jim, some of his choices led to his untimely death. This is highly ironic as well. I do not judge Jim for his choices in terms of substance abuse. There is a direct connection with creativity and self-medicating. Friends used to say he would often drink to simply quiet the voices from the spirit world he was constantly hearing. These are the same voices that gave him his greatest lyrics, however. I do not believe Jim sold his soul to the devil to achieve fame. I actually believe the Holy Trinity was using him as a means of bridging the liberal audience with the conservative one through music.

What was very ironic and more than coincidental looking back on it now was that I was given an award by my English teacher (a great guy named Geoff Bean) in 1992 for being an all-American scholar based on a creative analysis I wrote comparing the novel *The Heart of Darkness* by Joseph Conrad with the movie *Apocalypse Now* by Francis Ford Coppola. I remember vividly looking at the taped up newspaper article in the hallway of my school with an accompanying black and white photo of my high school senior photo that said "All-American Scholar Named by Academy." As was the case in my paper I wrote in high school, I had a direct interest in understanding the Vietnam conflict. I actually had an uncle named Tom Cannon who served in Vietnam as a military police officer, but he was tragically murdered when I was only a year old. Tom came home from Vietnam and bought a party store in rural Ida, Michigan. One night the store was held up for a little more than fifty dollars cash, and Tom was shot and killed. The incredible irony was he survived two tours in Vietnam only to be murdered back home. I was immersed in Vietnam movies as a teenager because I wanted to find some kind of spiritual connection to my Uncle Tom. One of my favorites was the movie *Platoon* by Oliver Stone. I would often spend time wondering if Mr. Stone knew my uncle Tom from Vietnam. A photo of Thomas G. Cannon in his Army greens as a military police officer is below. I come from a proud military family background. My cousin David Cannon, also shown below, is a high-ranking US Army Special Forces Officer and big time Doors fan.

Photo: Vietnam veteran and my slain uncle Thomas G. Cannon.

Photo: My cousin David S. Cannon, military deputy at Program
Executive Office-Simulation, Training and Instrumentation, Orlando,
Florida, US Army—a huge Jim Morrison and Doors fan, coincidentally.

There is one fascinating element to the entire filming of the
movie *The Doors*, directed by Oliver Stone. It was almost prophesied
perfectly by Jim in his poem/song "Stoned Immaculate." In the
movie Oliver Stone shows an image of the actor Val Kilmer, who
played Jim Morrison in the movie, next to the image of a stone statue
of a Greek God. The implication was that Jim had, in effect, achieved
a deity status by becoming a "rock god" like one of the Roman or
Greek gods themselves. In his poem/song Jim writes, "Let me tell
you about heartache and the loss of god, wandering, wandering in
hopeless night. Out here in the perimeter there are no stars, out here
we is stoned immaculate." As my photos will show later in this book,
I do believe whenever Jim was out under the stars there were probably
solar events and stellar events up in the sky signifying his presence
in front of Saint Mary. The entire passage suggests Jim's Christian
background of seeking God himself through his art, and ironically,
twenty years after his passing, he was in effect "stoned immaculate"

into movie history and onto celluloid film by a film director named Oliver *Stone, stoned* also being a word for being high on marijuana. Was Jim predicting in this song/poem prophetically that he knew one day twenty years after his death he would be immortalized immaculately like a deity in a film directed by a man with the last name Stone? It is entirely fascinating to consider this possibility of precognition and another example that Jim was most likely tied directly in his writings to the Holy Spirit and Saint Mary.

Let me state right here and now that while there are many tremendous advantages to being Christian/Catholic, we also are dealing with a church that I believe to be extremely misguided at times. I for one am extremely liberal when it comes to gay rights and gay marriage. Unfortunately, we have a system in the Apostolic Catholic Church that I believe to be not only spiritually oppressive but also flat-out doctrinally false. I do not believe there exists any connection whatsoever between your ability to hear God's voice and your personal sexual orientation or sexual history. If this were true, then no one should trust any teaching from a church that systematically covered up child sexual abuse for decades. I am reminded of the Hozier song "Take Me to Church" that has the lyrics "Let me tell you my sins so you can sharpen your knife." Unfortunately, this is exactly my own experience with both the church and many people I have known that call themselves Christian at times. Jesus Christ himself would state flat out that this does not comply with the keys to the Kingdom of Be Love and Believe. I am extremely supportive of gay rights since Be Love and Believe is for all of mankind regardless of race, gender, status, or sexual orientation.

Below is a photo from my high school graduation in 1992 from Detroit Catholic Central High School. A news clipping of my All-American Scholar announcement is to the right of me in the background. At my graduation ceremony, one of the art teachers purposefully mispronounced my name as Mark Pinard in an effort to humiliate me. His grievance with me was that I was kicked out of his art class as a high school sophomore for laughing during class. As I said before, it is no fun being a son of Mary, as Jim could tell you if he were still living. I can remember coming home many, many nights in high school, taking showers after practices and weeping at how cruel the coaches and teachers of a professed Catholic school were toward me for no reason. This led to my own substance use issues and acting out against authority for many, many years.

Photo: Matthew Douglas Pinard taken at high school graduation in 1992. A newspaper clipping in background to the right reads "All-American Scholar Named by Academy." Coincidentally, to the left is a sketching of Saint Mary's Son (Jesus) praying in the Garden of Gethsemane before his capture and crucifixion.

The analysis I wrote comparing the book *Heart of Darkness* with the movie *Apocalypse Now* in high school concluded that the only way to successfully navigate this world from a spiritual perspective is to embrace the dark side without allowing yourself to go over the edge. "The horror, the horror" that Marlon Brando's character Colonel Kurtz spoke of was more of a self-realization of the moral terror of allowing oneself to live without a god and any moral code and thereby suffering the dire consequences of losing one's soul in exchange. I know exactly where Jim went wrong in his life. He abandoned his strict Catholic upbringing in exchange for pursuit of excess, hedonism, and paganism, in addition to extreme alcoholism and illicit drug use. Jim used to say, "I believe in a long, prolonged derangement of the senses." Unfortunately, this was also his downfall.

What was fascinating in my analysis of *Heart of Darkness* and *Apocalypse Now* was that I was in essence criticizing my past life as Jim while at the same time drafting a critical analysis of a movie that was rife with the same music that, ironically, I had helped to create as front man, being with Jim, for the musical band the Doors in the mid-1960s. The one thing we share in common is our middle name, which is Douglas. *Douglas* literally translates to "dark river." It is the dark side that the best art, music, and writing comes from, but it is also where you can lose yourself in addiction and godlessness. I guess you could call it God's little inside joke of the Holy Trinity. I was always told as a young man that "God works in mysterious ways." In this case he was more than making it known who was at work in the birth of myself and Jim. We both were coincidentally born at times when our nation was about to go to war and when peaceful protest through art and music and writing was necessary.

Having served in the US military myself, I have tremendous respect for men and women in uniform but very little respect for our political leaders who bend the truth to initiate needless military conflicts. I largely thank Mr. Oliver Stone for this perspective. I blame politics and a nation that underappreciates the sacrifices of our men and women in uniform who are quite sadly taking their lives by their own hands at the pace of over twenty suicides per day currently. This is very greatly weakening our country both spiritually and militarily. We have become a privatized military industrial complex for profit that we were all warned about by great presidents like Ike Eisenhower. I chose, regretfully, to join the military and serve my country at a very young age. I've paid an extremely large price for doing so in terms of post-traumatic stress issues; however, at the time I believed that for some reason, it was where Saint Mary wanted me to be, possibly so that I could understand what our veterans would be going through years later when suicide rates would increase greatly post Iraq War.

What was quite essential to my growth at a young age was my introduction to the Catholic faith. I was baptized, given first communion, and confirmed in the Roman Catholic faith. This book first and foremost is not to selfishly promote my own life as some shining example of what I believe is "the way" necessarily. Rather, it is simply an attempt to explain the spiritual realities of how any one human being can self-actualize their soul so that it becomes one with the actual spiritual kingdom of God, which is simply another dimension right here on this earth and in our skies. One benefit of being raised Catholic is what I believe to be profound spiritual protection by simply wearing a white cross and receiving regular Catholic sacraments. Don't get me wrong, I have many Chinese friends who are genuinely good people of the Buddhist faith. I also have friends who are nondenominational people of the Christian faith who are outstanding human beings. I believe we all go to the same light if we are good and die in darkness if we live in constant ignorance of others and needless selfishness or if we are out to purposefully harm others. I am not here to promote Catholicism over any one world religion; however, I do believe in Saint Mary and the Holy Trinity as the true Godhead of this world for myself.

Since I am a Catholic, I can say Jesus Christ does save and has saved me more than once. I can count five separate times I should have been killed in my life and somehow miraculously survived. I had two nearly fatal car accidents, a faulty hand grenade that nearly killed me in Basic Training, a plane crash that killed my flight instructor on a day I was supposed to be up in the plane with him, and a nearly fatal food poisoning that left me so dehydrated I nearly died from heart failure. The other thing I will say is that I truly believe that a regular reception of the Catholic holy sacraments, in particular placing holy water on your forehead, and also receiving regular sacraments of reconciliation and the sacrament of Holy Communion will not only prevent many negative things like unexplained illness and disease, but this will also accelerate your ability to receive and decipher communication from the spirit world. Most spirits are here to protect us and warn us of things coming down the pipeline we may not be aware of. I always explain that I believe God the Father sees "ahead of time." With that kind of power on your side, wouldn't it be nice to have been able to see a 9/11 event, for instance, in advance?

There are many prophecies that describe the return of Jesus Christ as "the New Rose, the New Wine, and the Rose of Sharon." I know that I am the "New Wine" that Jim wrote of. The prophecy deals with "turning old skins into new ones" and a "New Wine generation" of Christianity. It is entirely focused on how Jesus taught us to be reborn in him spiritually. Many of Jim's writing in both his music and his poetry were taken directly from the Holy Trinity itself. Jim was highly attuned to the Great Spirit or Holy Spirit in his music and his writing. My wife's name coincidentally is Carol Rose Kloss. She is the "New Rose." Her name meaning literally translates to "song, flower, and stem." Stem as in the rose stem with thorns that were woven to create the torturous crown of roses, or crown of thorns, worn by Jesus Christ at his crucifixion. The "Rose of Sharon" is a former classmate of mine and well-known Fox News commentator by the name of Father Jonathan Morris. Fr. Morris, whom I've known most of my life, is the son of a wonderful woman named Sharon. He is a brilliant and articulate priest who I believe should be our next pope one day.

Photo: Fox News commentator Father Jonathan Morris. A former classmate and a great spiritual leader. I believe he may become pope one day.

Now, this is also an interesting point to make. Both Fr. Jonathan and my wife Carol are extremely powerful entities in the Catholic kingdom. Carol is very clairvoyant, and I would imagine Fr. Jonathan is as well. The mantra is "Now we are three." Three again to signify the Holy Trinity and the new leaders as the New Rose, the New Wine, and the Rose of Sharon. The plan and design ahead of time were to provide three potential spiritual leaders should something happen to any one of us. This was necessary because we live in a day and age where the Dark One is winning the battle daily and the threat of an entire planet extinction level event (ELE) either through nuclear war or natural disaster is very prevalent. Saint Mary has been desperately trying to reunite all the folks who were initially a part of the Word of God and Sword of the Spirit Communities in the 1960s-1980s for this very reason. As Jim said in the song "Five to One," we are strong spiritually in numbers. The sad part is we tear each other down spiritually constantly. I see it time and time again in my own family, at my work, and in the community. My book here will be attacked as heresy most fervently from my own Christian Right family unfortunately. It will most likely be my secular friends who actually will believe my claims. It is the sad irony that casts a shadow on many organized religions. If everyone only knew "we are all one body," then the grasping and accepting of the second kingdom key of Believe will be easier to contemplate.

The rose flower itself is extremely important in the Catholic faith. For instance, after Jesus Christ was crucified he rose after three days after being dead. The number three is also extremely important in the Catholic faith. There are three persons of the Holy Trinity. Jesus rose after three days following his crucifixion. At a Catholic Mass, a bell is rung ceremoniously three times. Three is also an extremely important number in my story as the third one of Mary's sons. I was born in 1974, three years after Jim Morrison died in 1971. In the Doors song "A New Awakening" from the album *An American Prayer*, Jim chants that "blood is the rose of mysterious union." I guess you could jokingly say Jim *rose* from his death and opened his own door in 1974. He is suggesting the symbol of the Catholic rose being the unifying power of a flower that binds the Christians/Catholics to one another in both life and death through the blood of Christ and the rose flower. Just as Jesus Christ rose from the dead, so death is ultimately conquered through the blood of Christ and is symbolized with the rose flower. As such, the following image depicts Saint Mary, the mother of Jesus, with a rosary around her neck. The point of all of this is that every single human being has the capacity to be a part of "the body of Christ." Every single human being has the spiritual potential to become a noted saint like Saint Mary. Saint Mary was human herself and not even a half deity, and look at the power she has in the afterlife. We can all attain such a status in the kingdom, but only if we focus on the kingdom keys of "Be Love" and "Believe" in our fellow man.

Photo: Saint Mary, the holy mother of God, holding
the Baby Jesus and wearing a rosary.

So who is Saint Mary? She is the mother of Jesus Christ, the first Son. She was fully human. This is an important point to make. Mary was fully human and yet is now a very powerful saint present in our skies above who can appear as an apparition in spirit as my photo later will prove. So what does that tell us as humans about every one of our abilities to transform spiritually on this plane and the next? While the official church doctrine is that Jesus was a miraculous virgin birth, there is an abundance of recent evidence that suggests Jesus Christ had numerous other brothers and sisters from Saint Mary and Saint Joseph born under normal circumstances. In fact a recent grave of a direct half brother named James, brother of Jesus, has been unearthed, and his remains have been scientifically tied to Jesus's bloodline. Even modern fiction works such as *The Da Vinci Code* have suggested that Jesus Christ himself may have actually been married to Mary Magdalene—who was not, in fact, a prostitute as the Bible suggests.

My point is that with such varying tales throughout the ages as to who Jesus was and how he came and left this earth, how can anyone truly trust as 100 percent fact what any particular scripture or denominational church teaching tells us. Personally, I suspect there may have been an actual Jesus Christ bloodline. I believe it is highly likely that this bloodline was French. It would explain my spiritual abilities and the tie-in to my last name of Pinard (which is French slang for wine, as I stated earlier). What we do know is Jesus Christ was a great spiritual teacher and guide and truly was the Son of God. This is an important point, however. We all are truly sons and daughters of God. We all have spirits and the potential to do amazing things with them. In any denomination of Christian faith, Saint Mary is undisputedly the mother of the Son of God. She is also an extremely powerful Catholic spirit with incredible abilities to influence weather, generate earthquakes, and initiate miraculous healings. Currently, she is causing at least one major earthquake per day in the world to simply say "Wake up and listen once again to my three sons." The spiritual flip side of this powerful wrath is miraculous healing. It is being done to simply show there is a higher power above who truly runs this planet and it is not mankind. I have heard stories of human Catholic saints being able to levitate and perform bilocation, i.e., being in two different places at the same time. I personally have never witnessed this, but don't doubt it is possible through the Holy Trinity. Like the Catholic saying goes, "Through him, with him, and in him, in the unity of the Holy Spirit."

I do share a number of very key creative similarities with Jim Morrison. While I admit I don't look much like him now in my present forties as much, we looked very similar in our youths, i.e., high school years. Jim was notably able to change his physical appearance throughout his very young life in a pretty dramatic way. In his song "The Changeling," Jim knew quite well what he could channel spiritually and how accepting his body as a portal to the spirit world is. His outward physical features changed quite a bit throughout times in his young life. My ability to write similar poetry and be able to hit every single note almost exactly on key that he was able to hit in a recording studio are also similarities. I have little desire to leave this earth in the way he did, but do not judge him for his choices. He lived in a different era prior to things like twelve-step programs for substance addiction. Even though I am a professionally trained theater actor, I have tremendous social anxiety and stage fright and could never weather the life on tour of a rock star, for instance. I'm also terrified of needles and hard drugs and heavy alcohol. I've seen too many great talents die at the hands of drugs and alcohol. As the "New Wine," my only vice is an affinity for white wine. I choose to live a very simple and largely private life in pursuit of completing Saint Mary's and my Father's wills that are now left to be done here on earth with, hopefully, performing miracles of healing through faith. This is my gift to give to the world.

Jim was often referred to as a rock god. I believe he became self-aware of his true spiritual identity right before he died. In 1969 at the now infamous concert in Miami, he was photographed holding a lamb. The lamb is a symbol of Jesus Christ as a sacrifice for sin. A recent book was just published also suggesting Jim himself had quite a Jesus Christ fixation and complex. This, in my opinion, is because Saint Mary had found a way to merge their two souls together and then add mine, a third one, this past fall in October 2016. In the song "The End," Jim sings about "the ancient lake," which is a reference to Lake Michigan where this spiritual fusing would take place in the skies near Grand Haven, Michigan. In this same song about "the end" (which coincidentally was featured in the movie *Apocalypse Now*), Jim also sings, "Ride the snake, to the lake, the ancient lake, baby, the snake he's long, seven miles, he's old, and his skin is cold." Jim also talks about kissing the serpent/snake on the tongue.

Allow me to decipher the metaphors from a Catholic perspective. Again, the ancient lake is a reference to Lake Michigan. The serpent who is seven miles and who is old and whose skin is cold is a direct reference to me and my incarnation of being Jim and our combined ages of seventy years old by the time of this publication on my birthday of February 26, 1974. The "skin is cold" is a reference to my current circulation problems I have with both my hands and feet because I am a seventy-year-old man in some respects. Many have touched my feet and hands before and mentioned how cold they are. That is essentially because I am seventy years old and I am also Jim who is technically dead physically. The serpent in the Bible is a sign of the devil, who first gave Adam and Eve the "apple of knowledge" and was summarily kicked out of the Garden for this. What Jim is saying is neither he or I are the devil at all. Kiss the snake—we are sons of Mary; trust and believe in us. As such Jim also sings in "The End," "It hurts to set you free, but you'll never follow me." He's basically saying, "I tried to redeem you eternally, but you did not follow, but it still pains me to set you free." Jim is saying, "If you reject me, you cannot enter the kingdom, and it hurts me to not be able to save you." Many also described Jim's prosecution in Miami as a public crucifixion that eventually led to his death. The conviction has since been overturned, but the damage was done nonetheless. Many said the Miami trial is what sent Jim into a spiral in Paris with heavy drugs that he just could not pull himself out of. In his infamous song "When the Music's Over," he screams in agony through the speakers,

"Jesus, save us!" He was crying out. He somehow prophetically knew his time was nearing an end on this earth, and he was most likely not aware of his pending reincarnation. I do know that Jim was aware his lyric and poetry would serve as spiritual guides for the world and also as "markers" for me to pick up his mission where he left off. Jim's poem "An American Prayer" was his hope for world peace, his own spiritual salvation, and a prediction of when Christ's kingdom would return.

I do now completely believe Jim was merged spiritually with the Son of God and the Lamb in Jesus Christ as the second son of Saint Mary. Don't get me wrong. I believe every human being is ultimately forged in God's own image with a soul and a potential to achieve the ability to perform miracles through Saint Mary. Jim was extremely special and different than most. His IQ was far beyond most, and his ability to write poetry and lyrics and sing is something directly from up above. At some point, I believe out in the desert with Pam, John, Robby, and Ray while dropping acid is where Jim first encountered the true Holy Spirit and realized his mission through Saint Mary. In fact, below are some still frames from Oliver Stone's Doors movie that are highly suggestive of Jim Morrison's true spiritual nature and awakening in this regard.

In the Doors movie from 1991, there is a pivotal scene where Jim, Pam, John, Robby, and Ray are out in the desert dropping acid for the first time. It is when the filmmaker suggests this event occurred. It may have been when he accepted the Holy Spirit in and perhaps Jesus Christ and Saint Mary as well. This scene suggests this is not only where Jim encountered the Great Creator spirit for the first time, but Oliver Stone also shows the audience a frame that when only Jim himself is walking alone out in the desert, the entire sun is eclipsed by the moon. This suggests that Mr. Stone is implying Jim's presence outdoors had an influence on Saint Mary, the Holy Father, and the Holy Spirit, causing the solar eclipse in our environment. It is a sly, quick veiled inference by a highly skilled and seasoned dramatic film director in Mr. Stone.

Photo: This above photo of a solar eclipse is similar to the shot Oliver Stone uses in the film The Doors to suggest that Jim's presence in the environment was signaled in the heavens above by the Holy Trinity.

Jim's mission was to provide the world with the polar opposite of the needless war and violence of Vietnam. Jim's own father ironically was commander of the US naval vessel that was directly involved in the Gulf of Tonkin incident which has now, like weapons of mass destruction and the Iraq War, been proven to be a staged event to lure our country into a senseless war for profit. My master's degree thesis from Louisiana State University entitled "The American and South Vietnamese Pacification Efforts During the Vietnam War" expressly delves into how, as Oliver Stone once stated, "America was eating itself in that war." The United States was attempting to initiate two conflicting military strategies at the same time with drastic results. It is the military industrial complex run amok that we were warned about as a nation by Ike Eisenhower before he left office. Jim stated on numerous occasions that the Doors fans and music industry executives only "want my death." He famously predicted being the third rock star from that era to die at the young age of twenty-seven years old, joining Janis Joplin and Jimi Hendrix in that notorious group of tragic overdoses. The following photo shows a photograph from the infamous 1969 Miami concert where Jim is holding a lamb onstage:

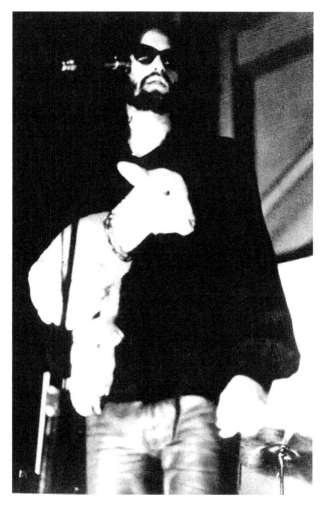

Photo: Jim Morrison as lead singer of the Doors at the infamous 1969 Miami concert where he was arrested for indecency and public exposure. Jim is holding a lamb for a photo. The lamb is a Christian symbol for Jesus Christ.

So why was Jim Morrison quite possibly the second lamb or second son of Mary? Well, it's quite fascinating if you really delve into his poetry. His poem "An American Prayer" is laden with Christian/Catholic imagery and is quite prophetic in describing the modern times of 2016 when the Christian kingdom would return. Let's take a close look at this underexamined masterpiece:

An American Prayer

by James Douglas Morrison

Do you know the warm progress under the stars?
Do you know we exist?
Have you forgotten the keys to the Kingdom?
Have you been born yet & are you alive?
Let's reinvent the gods, all the myths of the ages
Celebrate symbols from deep elder forests
[Have you forgotten the lessons of the ancient war]
We need great golden copulations
The fathers are cackling in trees of the forest
Our mother is dead in the sea
Do you know we are being led to slaughters by placid admirals
& that fat slow generals are getting obscene on young blood
Do you know we are ruled by TV
The moon is a dry blood beast
Guerrilla bands are rolling numbers in the next block of green vine
Amassing for warfare on innocent herdsmen who are just dying
O great creator of being grant us one more hour to perform our art & perfect our lives
The moths & atheists are doubly divine & dying
We live, we die & death not ends it
Journey we more into the Nightmare
Cling to life our passion'd flower

Cling to cunts & cocks of despair
We got our final vision by clap
Columbus' groin got filled w/ green death
(I touched her thigh & death smiled)
We have assembled inside this ancient & insane theatre
To propagate our lust for life & flee the swarming wisdom
  of the streets
The barns are stormed
The windows kept & only one of all the rest
To dance & save us
W/ the divine mockery of words
Music inflames temperament
(When the true King's murderers are allowed to roam free a
  1000 magicians arise in the land)
Where are the feasts
We were promised
Where is the wine
The New Wine
(dying on the vine)
Resident mockery give us an hour for magic
We of the purple glove
We of the starling flight & velvet hour
We of arabic pleasure's breed
We of sundome & the night
Give us a creed
To believe
A night of Lust
Give us trust in
The Night
Give of color
Hundred hues
A rich Mandala
For me & you & for your silky pillowed house
A head, wisdom & a bed
Troubled decree

Resident mockery
Has claimed thee
We used to believe in the good old days
We still receive In little ways
The Things of Kindness & unsporting brow
Forget & allow
Did you know freedom exists in a school book
Did you know madmen are running our prison
W/in a jail, w/in a gaol, w/in a white free protestant
Maelstrom
We're perched headlong
On the edge of boredom
We're reaching for death
On the end of a candle
We're trying for something
That's already found us
We can invent Kingdoms of our own
Grand purple thrones, those chairs of lust
& love we must, in beds of rust
Steel doors lock in prisoner's screams
& muzak, AM, rocks their dreams
No black men's pride to hoist the beams
While mocking angels sift what seems
To be a collage of magazine dust
Scratched on foreheads of walls of trust
This is just jail for those who must
Get up in the morning & fight for such unusable standards
While weeping maidens show-off penury & pout ravings for a
        mad staff
Wow, I'm sick of doubt
Live in the light of certain
South Cruel bindings
The servants have the power dog-men & their mean women
Pulling poor blankets over our sailors
(& where were you in our lean hour)

Milking your moustache?
Or grinding a flower?
I'm sick of dour faces
Staring at me from the TV
Tower. I want roses in my garden bower; dig?
Royal babies, rubies must now replace aborted
Strangers in the mud
These mutants, blood-meal
For the plant that's plowed
They are waiting to take us into the severed garden
Do you know how pale & wanton thrillful
Comes death on strange hour
Unannounced, unplanned for like a scaring over-friendly
guest you've brought to bed
Death makes angels of us all & gives us wings where we had
shoulders smooth as raven's claws
No more money, no more fancy dress
This other Kingdom seems by far the best until its other jaw
reveals incest & loose obedience to a vegetable law
I will not go
Prefer a Feast of Friends
To the Giant family

So from this great American work of poetry we have some very crucial markers of exactly what Jim was trying to prophesy and pray for. First of all, take close note of Jim's multiple uses of *we're*, as in "we are." Now this could be a reference to all of man as a collective "we are" like in his song "The Universal Mind"; however, it is also a veiled reference to Jim and Matt and Jesus being collectively fused as three spirits in one body in the fall of 2016. He is speaking directly in this poem to both America and the Holy Trinity of which he represented one third of, the Son of God. He speaks of **"keys to the kingdom, great golden copulations, our mother is dead in the sea, fat generals getting obscene on young blood, we are ruled by T.V., an insane theatre, the purple glove, the new wine, we of sundome** and night, give us a creed to believe, reaching for death on the end of a candle, a T.V. Tower, roses in the garden bower, royal babies, and another Kingdom that seems by far the best until the other jaw reveals incest and loose obedience to a vegetable law."

At first glance this all seems like complete nonsensical utterings of an alcohol- and drug-addicted, overly flamboyant and pretentious rock star. Upon further unraveling and inspection, you will see the entire poem itself is a completely prophetic prayer that will directly point to his next reincarnation as well as signal when the gates of the new kingdom would be opened in the fall of 2016. Allow me to explain. Jesus, in the first Son incarnation, gave two keys to Saint Peter to open the gates of heaven. These were not literal golden keys as depicted in many illustrations like the one below, rather they are metaphors for how to enter heaven eternally:

Illustration: Jesus Christ handing the keys of the kingdom to Saint Peter.

Nowhere in the Catholic dogma does it ever explain what exactly the two keys are supposed to represent. The keys are two simple guides for living in this side of life and being granted entrance into the kingdom of heaven when one dies. The first key is to simply "be love" and the second key is to "believe." It's quite simple: if you love your fellow man and simply believe in the existence of the Holy Trinity you will enter the kingdom after you die. I have been since fortunate to enter the kingdom prior to death, and I will demonstrate in this book how this is possible.

So let's decipher some more of Jim's "An American Prayer." He also says we need "great golden copulations, that our mother is dead in the sea."

Jim is directly referring here to nonvirgin births of half human, half deities that are directly from Saint Mary's garden or her sea. He says this again in the poem when he states "I want roses in my garden bower." Here he is prophesying the births of the "New Rose" and "Rose of Sharon" and the "Purple Rose," who is also a female half deity born of a friend of mine who is also French. Great "golden copulations" is how the Holy Trinity infuses new deities into this world, using two human parents through a nonvirgin birth. Yes, I will say this again, it is quite possible to bring a half-human, half-deity Roman Catholic soul into this world without a virgin birth. It's actually the only way. Let's be honest, every human conception of any child is a miracle in and of itself. I have an old friend who just had a daughter graduate high school whose name is coincidentally "Rose" that I believe is a half deity from Saint Mary. She is Jesus's "Purple Rose." Mary has a definitive succession plan for her "royal babies" that Jim prayed for in "An American Prayer." I will go even further to suggest that anyone baptized, confirmed, and given Holy Communion and receives regular Catholic sacraments and answers the daily call of Saint Mary can become a Catholic saint with spiritual powers beyond anything imaginable. This is also a call by Saint Mary to identify the next spiritual leaders of this world following the eventual deaths of "The New Rose, New Wine, and Rose of Sharon." These are the children of Saint Mary being born every day in this world. They may not even be being raised Catholic at the moment. That is okay with her. She is saying everyone is invited to the relationship with the Holy Trinity.

Let's look more closely again at the rest of the poem. Jim talks of **"fat generals getting obscene on young blood, we are ruled by T.V., an insane theatre, the purple glove, the new wine, we of sundome and night, give us a creed to believe, reaching for death on the end of a candle, a T.V. Tower, roses in the garden bower, royal babies, and another Kingdom that seems by far the best until the other jaw reveals incest and loose obedience to a vegetable law."**

Again, a lot of this seems nonsensical. However, when you begin to decipher it, you will see most of this points directly to my own arrival as the third son to be revealed in the fall of 2016 and the world conditions at the time. For instance, "fat generals getting obscene on young blood." At the time Jim wrote this, the United States was still involved in Vietnam and had lost nearly fifty thousand soldiers in that war. In 2016, the United States again was embroiled in another Vietnam-like war in the Middle East that saw tens of thousands of casualties. There are also an unprecedented twenty military veterans per day committing suicide. "We are ruled by T.V." in this generation as Jim's generation was. Jim also talks about an "insane theatre" and the "purple glove." These are both references to my professional theater background and training. In 2002, I was a writing apprentice for Jeff Daniels, the famous Hollywood A-list actor and his Michigan-based Purple Rose Theatre Company. The "purple glove" is a direct reference to the royalty of a king in a kingdom (the color purple) and also the Purple Rose Theatre company (this insane theater) in the glove state of Michigan.

While serving as an apprentice at The Purple Rose Theatre Company in Chelsea, Michigan, we were required to attend all the formal workshops. We had one particular workshop that was an introduction to acting and using papier-mâché masks of our own faces to do what was called mask work. An incredible woman and phenomenal actress named Michelle Mountain led these workshops with another amazing actress and friend named Sandy Birch. (Catch both of them at local theater shows in the purple-glove state of Michigan.) One of the exercises we had in this class was called the "ball of light" exercise. In this exercise you were told to lie completely flat on your back and imagine a ball of light as you closed your eyes. It was a very meditative exercise meant to hone your instinctual acting skills. I distinctly remember while doing this exercise and focusing on the ball of light the sensation of actually leaving my physical body. I remember the sensation of flying and my spirit leaving my physical form. It was quite a spiritually transcendent experience.

Let's look more at some of the stanzas from the poem written by Jim prior to his untimely death. Jim talks about **"we of sundome and night, give us a creed to believe, reaching for death on the end of a candle and another Kingdom that seems by far the best until it's other jaw reveals incest and loose obedience to a vegetable law."** This is where things get a little more complicated. In 2016 the gates of heaven were cracked open by Saint Mary and myself, her third son, with the prophetic help of son 2, Jim Morrison. It is a kingdom of sundome. Think about this for a minute. The Son of Saint Mary is also "the Son and Sun of Saint Mary." Yes, Catholicism, similar to some of the Egyptian sun religions is based on Saint Mary, the Holy Trinity, and the sun in the sky. In order to have a viable planet on earth thriving with life, you need a solar power in the form of a sun to facilitate evolution. This is what God the Father created when he said, "Let there be light." My photos will demonstrate what I mean by this. In order to enter the kingdom here on earth, you simply have to be love and believe. These are the keys—thus the line from Jim's poem, "Give us a creed to believe."

Now, here's my favorite line from Jim's "An American Prayer": "We're reaching for death on the end of a candle" and also being "perched headlong on the edge of boredom." Jim is referring to both himself and me after the gates were cracked open being able to connect spiritually and psychically through prayer and our mental and emotional states at the time of this event. When I pray to Saint Mary, I always place my palms above the candle to warm the wounds of Jesus Christ, the first Son, in my hands. The "reaching for death" part simply means we are both wounded, tired, and hurting and we miss our connection to the kingdom by being still in human form here on earth. When I touch the statue after doing this ritual, it is rare that she ever denies my prayer request, or at the very least delivers what I need instead of what I simply want. I have no clue why I started doing this, but for some reason it works. Now the final lines that refer to this new kingdom are "this other Kingdom seems by far the best until it's other jaw reveals incest and loose obedience to a vegetable law." This one took me quite a while to grasp. He again is referring to the new Sun King in my own third incarnation of the son of Saint Mary. Jim used to say "I am the Lizard King." What I am as the third son is actually a "sun king" of the Sundome or New Sun/Son Kingdom. Jim was also a sun king but thought he was a lizard king. Spiritually speaking, a lizard king "sheds its skin" spiritually speaking, and this allows for eternal life through Catholic sacraments and devotion.

Another Doors song titled "Indian Summer" also hints at the coming of the kingdom in the fall of 2016 as it was an Indian summer, which is a weather phenomenon whereby the fall or autumn weather is unseasonably warm. The fall of 2016 in West Michigan was a highly unusually warm autumn, unlike any I've ever seen in the Midwest my entire life. In fact most the photos below of the glowing sunsets and sun's golden rays were taken in mid- to late October and mid-November. We actually had a day recently in January where it was an unusual sixty degrees. Pay attention to the lyrics of this Doors classic "Indian Summer," where Jim sings, "I love you, the best, better than all the rest, That I meet in the summer, Indian Summer." He speaks of a "meeting" in an unusually warm autumn. Is this when he and I were be finally merged, our souls now one in Jesus Christ in the fall of 2016? Is this when the New Sun would appear in the skies of West Michigan? It is yet another Doors song that is intriguing and suggests Jim was certainly tied into the Great Creator Spirit or Holy Spirit.

The reference to the other kingdom seeming by far the best until the other jaw reveals incest is a direct reference to my own spiritual identity as a son of Mary being potentially unaccepted by the Catholic Church in 2016 due to scandal. The "other jaw" refers to my actual right side jaw, in which I actually have severe TMJ or lockjaw from an event in my youth. Think about what a jaw does mechanically. It talks and eats and sings and preaches. Jim was Saint Mary's other "jaw" through his clairvoyant and prophetic poetry and musical lyrics. He was speaking for the Holy Trinity. Jim refers to this jaw metaphor again on the American Prayer album. In the song "To Come of Age," he states, "Can we resolve the past, lurking jaws, joints of time?" This has highly specific prophetic relevance to the kingdom being unlocked in the fall of 2016. The "Can we resolve the past" directly referring to myself and an old friend whom I will call Saint Peter sitting down together. The "lurking jaws" refers to Jim's and my own "voices" of Saint Mary, speaking on her behalf. In my opinion, he is directly referring to when the New Wine (myself) would "come of age" on the vine of Christ, metaphorically and spiritually speaking, and when he and I would be fused as "lurking jaws" that literally transcend the "joints of time." It is when we would "become one in three" through the return of the Christian kingdom and also when I would finally put together how the album *An American Prayer* is more than a prayer, it is a return of the Christian kingdom prophecy.

I suspect Jim Morrison eventually knew this to be truly possible only through a return to Christianity and the Holy Trinity, even though he claimed he gained his own spiritual abilities only after witnessing a major traffic accident with Navajo Indians in his youth. I myself am actually part Cherokee Indian. I am proud of my heritage. It is also, in addition to my Catholic faith, what makes me very spiritual myself. Even the Native Americans believed in the Great Spirit. Many Native American rituals were very similar to Catholic rituals at church. It is shameful and ironic that the white Christian powers in the 1800s-1900s were also responsible for decimating this incredible race of the first true Native Americans of this country. It also speaks volumes that a non-Christian religion of Native American shamanism can also be a profoundly powerful and prophetic entrance into the spirit world. Catholicism teaches this "necromancy" of speaking with the deceased is largely of a demonic nature and that sometimes darkness masquerades as light in these communications. I would certainly agree that some very deceptive evil spirits may try to do this. However, my communications with Saint Mary have been of a nature of trying to warn against doom and trying to heal the sick. Would Lucifer himself be able to cloak himself and come to us as Saint Mary to prevent war and death? I very much doubt even the devil's ability to manipulate a spirit as strong as Saint Mary to this degree.

When I was nineteen years old, I was called to testify by the State of Michigan against a very dangerous pedophile in my neighborhood who had sexually assaulted two local underage girls after plying them with alcohol. He was also a Christian deacon at his church that was of a non-Catholic denomination. Coincidentally, this man's name was Lou Warden. I always found this to be peculiar. *Lou* could refer to "Lucifer" or "Satan." His last name was extremely interesting as he was found guilty and sentenced to prison. A prison is run by a *warden*. My right jaw is severely TMJ'd from the entire stress of the experience of testifying and feeling afraid I may have to encounter him again one day. Mr. Warden was a highly trained Special Operations Marine who had seen multiple tours in Vietnam, and I have no doubt may have also killed women and children in the war. He was by far one of the most dangerous individuals I have ever encountered. He was a true wolf in sheep's clothing. I have since been an ardent opponent of pedophilia in the priesthood in the Catholic Church and have suffered alienation and condemnation from both my own Catholic high school and numerous Catholic friends and family since this event from my youth. It has caused severe anxiety and depression in me for decades. I may not be accepted by the Catholic hierarchy as anyone of any significant spiritual importance simply for these reasons alone. What is also of an interesting note and also of a prophetic nature is Jim mentions on the album *An American Prayer* meeting "two young girls" in his lyrics. Did he have some precognition of this event involving my neighbor and the two young female victims somehow? It is interesting to consider this possibility.

At the age of twenty-two years old, I rather impulsively joined the US Army as a qualified legal specialist to pay for my college degree from the University of Michigan. I'll never forget my first day in the entrance processing station also called MEPS. On your way to Basic Training, they ship all of the recruits on very large blue school buses onto the bases. When I recall this very strange image, I can't help but remember the lyrics from the Doors song "The End." Jim sings, "The blue bus, is calling us, the blue bus, is callin' us, driver where're you taking us?" Is this Jim being able to see into the future when he and I, now possibly joined as souls, are entering Basic Training together as he refers to my incarnation as the New Wine? The possibility is incredibly mysterious. It is as if he's almost "cracked the code" between time and space, memory, present existence, and the living and how it all interacts synergistically with the spirit world. And somehow, amazingly, he knew I would eventually put it all together coherently one day, and it would lead to the gates of heaven being cracked wide open with Saint Mary's divine assistance.

Another very interesting line from the same Doors song of "The End" refers to the West. Jim sings, "The West is the best, The West is the best, get here and we'll do the rest." What is very interesting is Jim's music career didn't take off until he left Florida for Los Angeles, California, on the West Coast. Also, if referring to the future spiritual event of the gates of heaven being cracked open in West Michigan in the Fall of 2016 near Grand Haven, the lyrics also are hypnotically prophetic, "The West is the Best, get here and we'll do the rest." Who is the *we'll* in this line? Is it Jim and I? Is it Jim and Saint Mary? The "get here and we'll do the rest" suggests a longing perhaps for spiritual and or physical healing that will be done by Catholic deities? The possibilities are endless.

Now here is another interesting part of Jim's poem. He talks about the new kingdom showing a "loose obedience to a vegetable law." This is a direct reference to the times in 2016 in the United States where there would be many false allegations of people and false prosecutions of those of the Christian faith through police and the justice system. To date I have seen a high school friend's sister be sentenced to twenty-three years in prison for a crime I do not believe that she committed, and I myself was recently threatened with absurd stalking charges that authorities admitted would never meet the threshold for a criminal charge simply for attempting to leave a Catholic rosary with a sick friend's wife who has cancer in an attempt to help heal her. I was being persecuted and threatened with prosecution for attempting to do a Christian deed and heal the sick. Jim almost predicted such events to a tee. I'm going to now post below my own poem, written this year, that is an extension of "An American Prayer" and show how current events seem to pick up where Jim's prophecy left off:

An American Prayer, Continued

By Matthew Douglas Pinard

Memoriam James Douglas Morrison

Saint Peter, my friend, I proclaim to see
Two keys to our Kingdom now will be
For they shall be love and believe
Dropped down from a cloaked hand in purple sleeve

For I am the lamb and the son, now there are three
The dark river skinned moor, the second was he
Now a new wine, old skins into new ones, God's gift shall be
For I am the King, James, and he is now in me, three years after he

We're both placing praying palms above candles lit for she
My mother's red soaked en-cloaked face appears for me
A triple headed moon a self crowning sun, fraternal twins
Roses from the garden bower above, two rainbows from her sea

THE NEW WINE

Two funerals to usher in a new sun forever now to be
Christina's new village and the tower locksmith was he
I touched his cold hand, his age ninety three
A single red rose adorned his crystal casketed ship for thee

I pray now for the aborted souls in the mud, this earth, this day
Twenty in Army Green, cold steel barrels to their heads now we see
Their mother and father who left them on the Cross
I scream now at the TV tower, at the senseless blood shed and loss

A yellow rose, a new wine, and the Rose of Sharon now alive
Born forever to be, the sun soaked wet rock of her pier
Of her Grand Haven, a heaven, revelations rays now piercing October's sky
In the glove hand state of his new Kingdom, now purple and free

She cracked open the gates, now the earth's crust doth shake
A single red heart of the Son, fault lines they do trace, the red brick
In the Chapel of Saint Joseph did I see, this miracle of his not faked
A yellow and red pinked hued fire did appear from the earth as she picked

Her name is both a song and a rose, and on the third day did he
A small pocked birthmark, left breast atop the cage is now on me
Like a spear from a Roman soldier pierced into his thoracic spine
Left hand, left numb, his right hand must now heal the world divine
Quis Et Deus, are you Godlike? For did we not see, nation rise up against nation

As in the good book that he had decreed
For whosoever that did believe, shall walk in his light eternally
A win for God's win, Randy, he taught me how to see, one foot now in each
Kingdom is possible to be, his ghost light doth shine forever on me

The feasts we were promised, red blood wine shed for you and me
A wooden chalice did he prepare, the steps walked firmly in he
Tattooed on his back, a yellow rose, one pink, fraternal twins predict
The golden wrought iron gates, metaphorically released

For what was that crown that adorned upon his head
A German name for a stem, wound perfectly in three
Thorns adorn the King's crown remade, royal babies now be born
A stalk, stalking, loose obedience to his law has been seen

We of Sundome in the middle of the dark night, her light has been loosed
A purple silky pillow cased for the head now chimed in a steeple for three
His garden not be severed, the invisible now seen, the other Jaw incensed at incest
This other Kingdom is by far the best, the feast of friends now in he who is three
All for our mother to see

Photo: The image above directly reflects biological markers of one of two of my past life experiences. Notice this depiction is showing Jesus Christ being pierced by a Roman soldier on his right side of his rib cage. This is factually incorrect as many other similar depictions also show. The truth is Jesus Christ was pierced on his left side above his rib cage. The left side is where his heart would be, and it would have caused the red and white fluids to drain out of his heart, which is consistent with a piercing heart wound that would drain both blood and water from him. I coincidentally have a small birthmark atop my left rib cage.

A small pocked birthmark, left breast atop the cage is now on me
Like a spear from a Roman soldier pierced into his thoracic spine
Left hand, left numb, his right hand must now heal the world divine.

I have a small wound birthmark right above the left side of my rib cage. Depictions from the Bible talk of blood and water flowing out of the wound. This is reflective to a heart wound from the left side of the upper rib cage. I also as a young child had severe anxiety anytime I was near a Christian crucifix. I was particularly uncomfortable with the blood wounds on the statues where Jesus was crucified at his hands and feet and pierced by a Roman lance. Some illustrations show him being pierced on the right side in both statues and in drawings/ paintings like the image above. This is incorrect. Jesus was pierced on this left side where his heart was. I also suffered, due to a severe whiplash injury I received while on leave from active duty in the US Army, severe piercing pain straight through my thoracic spine in the middle of my back. This is consistent with what the pain from a spear-like wound that would have first pierced Jesus's heart then went straight into his thoracic spine. My left hand often goes numb from this injury, and my right hand is now what I use to pray to Saint Mary and to heal others from illnesses and injuries. Miraculously, I myself have been healed from over a decade long of excruciating pain from my whiplash injury. It is an injury that supposedly was degenerative and incurable since its location was in my thoracic spine. Let's also look at the line from my poem—"The dark river skinned Moor, the second was he," this directly refers to Jim Morrison (as in *Moor* and *son*) in my belief as being the second son and Lamb of God.

So how did I help crack open the gates of heaven in October's sky of 2016? It's quite a fascinating story really. I've always been fairly clairvoyant since a very young age, a highly attuned intuitive. (I dislike the word *psychic*.) However, in the fall of 2016, this ability started to heighten itself beyond anything I could have ever imagined. I literally started being visited by spirits of friends I had known that had passed on. One of them was an incredibly intelligent intuitive theater actor, playwright, and local TV actor named Randy Godwin.

Focus on the last name especially of "Godwin" and break it down, *God* and *win*. Randy had never even stepped foot inside a Catholic Church but somehow had the ability to communicate with me that transcended what science told me was possible.

What was extremely ironic about Randy's ability to come to me spiritually was he had passed away a few years ago from suicide. He had had some medical difficulties and suffered as do I from chronic pain. Now, what was also extremely interesting was I had had some experiences in the military that seemed like random events at the time. I was almost killed by a hand grenade in basic training. I had a live grenade that had a faulty pin in it. I had pulled the pin out halfway and could not get the rest of it out. In essence it started to "cook." The trainer in the bomb suit across from me ran up and grabbed it out of my hand and dropped it over the retaining wall. Two seconds later I heard a very loud explosion. The event to this day has given me moderate PTSD. The amazing thing was I had blocked this near-death event out for almost twenty years as if it had never happened.

Another event was when, as a trained Army legal specialist, I had to assist on a capital murder case as part of my US Army JAG contract with the government. The crime was extremely disturbing. You can read about it if you simply google the case *United States v PVT Peter Roukis*. An enlisted man (PVT Roukis) had come home to find his wife had been unfaithful. He lured her back to their home and then proceeded to drive two twelve-inch blades through her neck, nearly decapitating her in the process. I had to process the crime scene photos for trial. I also did not process this event very well psychologically and have had some lingering trauma from it. The trade off of both these events was my clairvoyant abilities were heightened greatly from experiencing them. Both events served to further increase my ability to receive spiritual communication.

While working on the Roukis murder trial, I was fortunate to meet the spiritual advisor for PVT Roukis who was none other than Sister Helen Prejean of the famed *Dead Man Walking* book and movie. She was gracious to take photos with our Army JAG office. She gratefully signed my copy of her book for me. I had mentioned to her that I had just finished writing a paper on her book and movie for a class at the University of Michigan in my undergraduate studies for my bachelor's degree in psychology in the mid-1990s. From a spiritual perspective, one of the most disturbing things about this case was the look on PVT Peter Roukis face prior to his trial. He had a look on his face like he had just woken up from a bad dream. It also reminded me of Jim's prophetic line from "The End" where he sang, "The killer awoke before dawn [before we cracked the gates open] and he put his boots [Army boots] on." It was as if Jim predicted this crime before it happened. It appeared to me that PVT Roukis spiritually was not in the driver's seat alone, so to speak, when this horrific crime occurred. To me that was more frightening than simply believing this one young man was 100 percent a total monster of violence and rage. I believe it is entirely possible he was possessed demonically at the time of the crime. A photo of Sister Helen Prejean is below. Sister Prejean is one of the most humble Catholics I have ever met.

Photo: Sister Helen Prejean, author of the book *Dead Man Walking*. Sister Prejean served as spiritual counselor to PVT Peter T. Roukis

in the Army capital murder case of *US v Roukis* at Fort Polk,
Louisiana, in 1997. I served as a US Army JAG legal specialist
on this case and processed the crime scene photos for trial.

Bob Daniels, father of famous actor Jeff Daniels, also started
to visit me regularly with Randy Godwin. Bob had recently passed
away a few years ago from a heart attack near my parents' lake house
on Cavanaugh Lake in Michigan. On one occasion Bob flashed
me an image of Jeff tuning one of his guitars from his wonderfully
famous unplugged shows. For some reason both Randy and Bob
came through clearest when I would be listening to Grateful Dead
music in my car. A particular favorite of theirs was the song "Ripple,"
which, if you pay close attention to the lyrics, gives valuable clues to
the other side of the kingdom as well. Bob and Randy had me focus
at first on the lyrics from "Ripple" of "Let it be known there is a
fountain that was not made by the hands of men." When I focused
on the word *fountain* he flashed me the name of my hometown of
Spring Lake, Michigan. *Fountain = spring*. He was saying there is a
fountain or spiritual source in the town of Spring Lake, Michigan,
not made by the hands of men (a deity). In a second instance, Bob
flashed me an image of the tuning fork Jeff used to tune his guitar
with before he played his unplugged shows. It was his way of saying
the "tuning" events from the military were not random at all. My
almost being killed by a hand grenade and then processing one of the
most violent murder scenes I've ever seen further tuned my ability
to receive spiritual communication from the spirit world in order to
help protect and warn my country.

Photo: Emmy winning actor and writing and acting mentor Jeff Daniels. Jeff hired me as an apprentice at his Purple Rose Theatre to write a Comedy Golf Jam for him in 2002. Jeff is the son of Bob Daniels, who peacefully passed away near my parents' yard. The entire Daniels family are a wonderful group of laid-back and loving Michiganders.

Bob and Randy were basically telling me that my body, mind, and soul were now a fine-tuned musical tuning fork of a much larger instrument—that being the entire spirit world. Bob Daniels passing away near my parent's yard on Cavanaugh Lake in Chelsea, Michigan, from a heart attack while jogging was not random at all in either the timing of the event nor the location. There is no random on this side, and it all serves a purpose. On the other side is the message Bob was distinctly giving me. Bob was also showing me he was in total peace and light yet still able to communicate with this side. What was also amazing about my episodes of communication with Randy and Bob was that they both came to me from the highest sources of light known to the universe. This told me he was with Saint Mary and not in any kind of purgatory or hell from how he had passed away as the Catholic Church sometimes teaches. In fact, Randy kept flashing me the word *opposite,* meaning the actual opposite of what we learn via Christian or Catholic dogma is actually true in the afterlife, especially as it pertains to things like suicides. He was also saying the opposite is true of how men and women judge each other in this life as being spiritually worthy or not. What I mean by this is that often we push the most spiritually worthy people to the edges or fringes of our society, either through a bogus judicial system or by excommunication from social groups or organized religious groups. There is a practice known as shepherding whereby a self-appointed leader will shepherd out anyone who opposes them or who shows any kind of higher ability to grow spiritually. This is a very dangerous practice for any human being to undertake in the name of God.

A hyper focus on sin is what further drives each of us to judge each other and cause division between us which further prevents any of us from entering the kingdom. It's about loving your neighbor and your enemy and believing in them as well as a Holy Trinity. People who commit suicide do not automatically go to a God-imposed hell. Randy came to me from the light and the kingdom for a few reasons. Mainly it was through Saint Mary, to help warn all of us of impending danger. Somehow on the other side you are able to see impending dangers ahead of time. Randy was warning me about a mutual friend's wife who had yet to be diagnosed with cancer. He told me to tell this mutual friend the words *ghost light.* He was trying to get my attention to try to help her and her family through prayer. When I gave this friend the words *ghost light,* he said it was the title of a television series he had been writing that he hadn't told anyone the name of. It was amazing. Randy had complete knowledge of something being privately worked on by a mutual friend who hadn't told anyone else what he was working on. We had another experience at our house where our dogs were barking incessantly at our ceiling in our bedroom. My wife said "It's some guy named Randy." She had never met Randy and did not know who he was.

Randy was also warning all of us about a very serious impending threat to all of mankind. About a week after he came to warn me of this impending threat, Russian president Vladimir Putin began putting ICBMs on the edge of Poland's border and began sending Russian destroyers through the English Channel to Syria. A week prior to this, the Russians bombed a UN convoy in Syria that greatly increased tensions in the Middle East between Russia and the United States. It was quite clear the world was closer to global thermonuclear war than it had been since 1962 and the Cuban Missile Crisis. I put together an e-mail with some of the photos I've enclosed below and sent out a warning to all my friends and family about the threat with Russia over Syria. It was amazing how few Americans were even aware how close to nuclear war we were with Russia in the fall of 2016. The KGB confirmed as much after our presidential election. I spent a long time in graduate school studying the Cuban Missile Crisis of 1962 and believe this education helped me see the signs of a potential impending nuclear conflict with Russia and helped me to warn family and friends via e-mail prior to our national election. There was no doubt Vladimir Putin helped to sway our national elections with his nuclear brinkmanship.

Right around the same time I had these incredible clairvoyant spiritual interactions with friends who had passed on, I was given an intuition from my local pastor named Fr. Dave at my local Saint Mary's Church in Spring Lake, Michigan. Fr. Dave said he wanted me to try to track down someone from my past as a youth whom I hadn't seen in many years. This man was also coincidentally named Peter. I refer to him now as Saint Peter because that is what Saint Mary is calling him now too, "the new Saint Peter." Saint Mary calls me her new son, and my old friend Peter is the new Saint Peter. Saint Peter was my Christian camp leader when I was in eighth grade and ran a ministry and television show called *Crossing the Goal*, which is a Christian-based sports-themed show combining football and Bible passages to formulate a game plan for men's spiritual lives. I have to admit, it's a great ploy to get men to watch a religious show since most men relate everything to sports. Saint Peter had a son named Joshua who was a star basketball player at West Point and was now on active duty as a second lieutenant. He also had a daughter named Rachel and other children I have not yet met. His wife (whom I will now call Saint Debbie) is a noted Catholic author herself who wrote a book called *Firmly on the Rock*, which I have recently read. Both I consider friends and well-respected theologians as well as amazing parents and people.

After meeting with Saint Peter a first time, I had a very profound experience in the middle of cornfields in Ionia, Michigan. I have a white silver cross that I had recently purchased for some unknown reason and "randomly" blessed at a church over thirty miles away in Holland, Michigan. The cross was blessed by a Fr. Bill at Saint Francis de Sales Church. Now the only connection I could immediately think of was my own father's name is Bill. The church itself is exceptionally beautiful, and it's the only one I've ever been inside of that has a wooden statue of Jesus Christ seated extending his hands out to his sides. The statue is situated so that young children can get their picture taken with Jesus. In any event, shortly after meeting with my old friend Saint Peter, I was driving in the middle of corn in Ionia, Michigan, when I had an intuition to pull the car over. Immediately I had sensations invading all five of my senses that I simply could not explain. I felt a prickly feeling, as if someone were drawing a crown around the rim of my head where a baseball cap would sit. This happened three times distinctly. In addition, a very bright white light filled the entire cab of my company car. It was nearly blinding and overwhelmingly warm and bright.

The only thing I can say is I had a distinct sensation of being in another dimension (the other kingdom). The rest of the day, I distinctly remember feeling being extremely light, as if walking on clouds. I called my friend Saint Peter and told him about the experience. He said, and I quote, "It sounds like Saint Francis de Sales." I proceeded to then tell him that my white cross had been blessed at Saint Francis de Sales Church in Holland, Michigan. This is why Saint Mary wanted me to visit with Saint Peter. Thankfully, Saint Peter and many other amazing adults of faith from the Word of God Community we were raised in taught us to discern the Holy Spirit from demonic influence and to not dismiss or ignore when we feel God is tapping us on the shoulder. The only word I came across in my studying online of what this experience may have been is *transfiguration*. The Bible teaches of how after Jesus Christ died and rose from the dead, he became transfigured in his spirit form in a radiant white light of glory. What is amazing is if this is indeed what I had experienced, which is what I believe did happen, it means you can transfigure in human form preceding physical death, rise up into the kingdom, and continue to live on both planes spiritually and physically prior to death.

Illustration: An artist's rendering of the transfiguration of Jesus Christ.

Shortly after this amazing experience, I had another strong intuition Saint Peter and I were supposed to meet again. We met a second time on a Thursday in October, which coincidentally is a holy day of sacred mysteries in the Catholic Church. In fact, Thursday is the day of the sacred mystery of the second coming of the kingdom and when Jesus was to hand the keys of the kingdom off to Saint Peter. Oddly enough, Saint Peter's wife, Saint Debbie, had started a movement through the Saint Mary's Church in Ann Arbor, Michigan, where my own birth parents were married and I was baptized. Saint Debbie's movement was called the "Be Love Revolution." Saint Debbie had nailed the first key to the kingdom all on her own.

On my way to meet Saint Peter for a second time, I was told by the Holy Spirit to stop off at a gas station on my way, and for some reason, I randomly bought two roses of opposite colors. One of the roses was yellow and one was pink. On my first date with my wife I brought her a yellow rose and did not know at that time her middle name was Rose. The pink rose is the same color of the rose of Sharon. On my way to meet Saint Peter, I was given an intuition from the Holy Spirit to turn my radio to the local Catholic EWTN station. When I did this, I heard two commentators discussing Rachel's fraternal twins from the Bible which I found to be an odd coincidence.

Upon meeting Saint Peter, I picked him up, and we visited my parents Church of Saint Mary's in Ann Arbor. We both sat and prayed a decade of Hail Marys in the pews. I handed him the flowers and the rosaries, and we departed on good terms. I told him I believed the Holy Trinity was trying to warn Americans about Vladimir Putin's intentions overseas. It was only on my way driving home that I realized I had picked up two twin roses that were opposite in color, thus "fraternal twins." The broadcast I had heard on the radio regarding fraternal twins was after I had purchased the fraternal twin roses. It was quite amazing to try to comprehend how amazingly powerful the Holy Spirit could be in this particular instance.

I drove home that afternoon and immediately was given a strong intuition to drive out to the edge of our local pier in Grand Haven,

Michigan. I stood on the edge of the pier as I watched with total and complete awe a large full-arching rainbow appear out of nowhere that went across the sky from one end of the channel to the other. I immediately recognized this as a possible sign of the biblical rapture. Many theologians associate the rapture with the concept of end times. End times does not necessarily mean the end of life on this planet as we know it. It could simply mean an end to secularism and Satanism and a return to the world's relationship with God through the Holy Trinity. A few minutes later, I was instructed to start driving north up to Ludington, Michigan. Within a few minutes, a second rainbow appeared in the sky. This rainbow was a half rainbow. It was the other "fraternal twin." It was still a rainbow, but was of different appearance than the other full rainbow, thus a fraternal twin. I kept driving. All of a sudden the sun appearing as a giant glowing bulb many times more brilliant and larger than any I had ever seen in my life cracked through the clouds, and golden rays shot right toward my car window.

Over the next few days, many more strange occurrences with the sun manifested. I have photos of the sun crowning itself. I have a photo of both the sun and the moon turning into triple-headed spheres to signify the Holy Trinity. In the song "Not to Touch the Earth" Jim sang "Sun, sun, sun" and "Moon, moon, moon." Sunsets with the entire sky turning deep hues of red and pink and yellow also appeared, as well as the sun with golden rays shooting at all angles across the sky. There is a photo of Lake Michigan with a fire-like red across the horizon, like a lake of fire. There are multiple photos with three separate multicolored orbs dancing around the sun. These different-colored orbs signify the three sons, the Holy Trinity, and the three spirits who initially came to me to teach me how to communicate directly with Saint Mary.

The most amazing of these photos, however, is a photo where there is clearly a veiled woman's face above the sun and the same sun later turning into a heart shape that was five times the normal size of the sun. I have never in my life ever seen anything like it before on this planet. It was my mother Saint Mary's way of signaling to the world who her new and third son was. I have enclosed many photos below as proof of the gates of heaven being cracked wide open in October 2016 in West Michigan.

Photo: A seagull cruises past the first full-sky rainbow over Grand Haven Pier in October 2016.

Photo: The second of "Rachel's fraternal twin" rainbows appears as a half rainbow in the sky of West Michigan in October 2016.

Photo: What I like to call the "new star" of West Michigan, or "new sun" of West Michigan, in the purple glove/hand state of God. Notice the three multicolored orbs that I believe signify the three spirits that initially visited me, the Holy Trinity, and Mary's three sons/suns.

Illustration: Imagine a string of Christmas lights strung together. This is how the spirit world is interconnected.

Picture in your mind the image of a Christmas tree with lights strung around the tree from top to bottom. This is essentially how the spirit world is interconnected. When spirits pass on in death, other spirits, friends, and family are there to greet them and "plug them into" the tree. Jesus Christ is often referred to as the "branch" of this tree. What I have found from my own life experiences is it is possible to "plug in" early before you depart this physical plane and receive spiritual communion with the dearly departed prior to physical death on this earth. This concept is clearly demonstrated in my photos of the new sun and the three differently colored orbs surrounding the rays of the sun.

Photo: The New Wine and the New Rose off the pier of Grand Haven in October of 2016. The sun is abnormally large and bright especially for mid-October in Michigan.

Photo: This miraculous red shaped heart with fault lines cracking the brick open can be found in Saint Joseph Catholic Church in Saint Joseph, Michigan.

On December 5, 2016, I entered the Chapel of Saint Joseph Catholic Church in Saint Joseph, Michigan, at approximately 1:30 p.m. EST. I walked up to the statue of Saint Mary in the photo below and placed my hands over two candles. I said three Hail Marys in front of the statue. Mary then said to me that she was going to then "crack open the earth." Within three minutes exactly, a 4.3-magnitude earthquake struck the coastline of Northern California. Since this date, every day there has been a magnitude 4- to 8-point earthquake at some location across the world. The headlines a few days later simply stated "The Ring of Fire Is On Fire." Yes, Saint Mary is quite capable of causing massive major earthquakes. She is simply trying to get the world's attention to usher in her new sun. The new sun is about protection and healing. It is not about judgment and condemnation. Sometimes Saint Mary has to go to extremes in order to get the world's attention that her three sons still walk the earth.

Photo: The Saint Mary's statue in Saint Joseph, Michigan, where she uttered "crack open the earth." Major, massive earthquakes from magnitude 4 to 8 have been hitting the entire planet since.

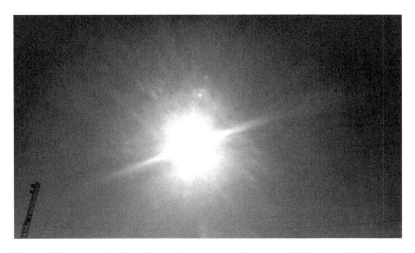

Photo: This remarkable photo above was taken at a Chicago toll booth on my way to help try to heal a friend's mother who was ill. You can see the veiled face of Saint Mary directly above the sun. Her veil even has a crease in it, and you can see her left eye socket and left cheekbone next to her nose. I have shown this photo in person to many people who also claim they see the exact same thing. Also present are the three multicolored orbs again.

Photo: This was an amazingly bright photo of the sun turning into three spheres and shining abnormally brightly. This was taken on my way home from Chicago after an attempt at a miraculous healing at a local Saint Mary's Parish. The sun was so bright and so big that I could not look directly at it at all. In the song "Not to Touch the Earth," Jim would sing "Sun, sun, sun."

Photo: The new moon turning into three spheres in the sky after a Sunday Mass at Saint Mary's Catholic Church in Muskegon, Michigan, in October 2016. In the Doors song "Not to Touch the Earth," Jim would sing "Moon, moon, moon."

Photo: This spectacular photo was taken on the end of Grand Haven Pier in Grand Haven, Michigan, days after the gates were cracked open. You can see the image of the sun crowning itself on top to signify a golden crown like the crown of a king on top of the new sun.

Photo: An amazing display of Saint Mary's beauty as "the sun's healing rays" shoot out from an abnormally bright sun in the middle of October in West Michigan in 2016.

Photo: "A lake of fire" appears on top of the surface of Lake Michigan in October 2016 off the coast of Grand Haven, Michigan.

Photo: An abnormally bright and radiant new sun shoots golden rays across the front of Saint Mary's Catholic Church in downtown Grand Rapids, Michigan, in October of 2016.

Photo: An incredible display of the new sun exploding into a yellow and orange fire as it sets off the pier of Grand Haven, Michigan, in October of 2016.

Photo: Moments after I asked Saint Mary to "crack open the gates" this sunset appeared near our home in Spring Lake, Michigan, in October of 2016.

Photo: This photo was again taken a day later after I again asked Saint Mary to "crack open the gates" on a Saturday afternoon in Spring Lake, Michigan, in October of 2016.

Photo: The new sun setting over Saint Mary's Catholic Church in Spring Lake, Michigan, in October 2016. You can see a statue of Mary holding a fallen Jesus in the background.

Photo: This highly abnormal sunset, like a fire from heaven, appeared near Saint Joseph, Michigan, after I had visited three local Catholic churches in October 2016 and left blessed rosaries in front of Marian statues.

Photo: This incredible display of the sky was taken off the coast of Muskegon State Park in late November of 2016. I believe it is Saint Mary giving a glimpse of the other kingdom through the clouds.

Photo: This incredible view of the new sun was taken early February 2017. You can see this new sun is here to stay. The fact the new sun is this bright in February is amazing. Notice the rays pointing to the two kingdoms—one above, one below— to signify the two related kingdoms of heaven and earth.

Photo: This amazing photo was taken of the new sun shining over the statue of Saint Mary holding Jesus in front of Saint Mary's Catholic Church in Spring Lake, Michigan. Notice again the three separate multicolored orbs. Also, notice the large golden halo that encircles the smaller globe of the new sun.

Photo: This incredible shot of the New Sun abnormally large and bright with multiple golden rays shining straight in front of Saint Mary's Catholic Church in Muskegon, Michigan.

Photo: The new sun vibrantly exploding like a nuclear detonation or like a fire from heaven over the Grand Haven coastline in October of 2016. This event happened right before the presidential election and Vladimir Putin's attempt to start a nuclear world war if Hillary Clinton had won the election. To me it was the dire warning from Saint Mary of the world being on fire.

Photo: The new sun being cut into two halves by a layer of clouds. Numerous people were on the beach taking photos and witnessing the new kingdom being born.

Photo: One of my favorite depictions of Saint Mary in the sky. Notice how her dress shows multiple depictions of a golden sun shooting healing rays outward.

Photo: The following amazing image of this highly abnormal cloud pattern right after a Catholic Mass at St. Joseph Catholic Church in St. Joseph, Michigan this March of 2017 shows what I would only be able to explain as Saint Mary's "Angels we have heard on high."

Photo: The New Rose and the New Wine out for a night of fun
on the town in Saugatuck, Michigan, in late fall of 2016.

Photo: One of my favorite photos of the New
Wine and New Rose out on the town.

Photo: The New Rose and New Wine in God's sky.

Photo: The New Wine and the New Rose on a wine and ski weekend in beautiful Cadillac, Michigan. I think this is one photo where I look a lot like Jim. I am also showing how I am a changeling.

Photo: The New Rose and New Wine on a West Michigan beach prior to the birth of the new sun.

Photo: Perhaps my favorite photo of the second son, Jim Morrison, with girlfriend Pam, date unknown. They seem happy and free. Jim mentioned once that he wanted to live to be a hundred years old. He and I are already seventy. While his death was tragic and untimely, he still is very much alive inside of me. His music and haunting lyrics will live forever. Jim used to tell his bandmates, "I'll be with you until the end of time."

Photo: The first Son, Jesus, and his Apostles at the Last Supper. As the second son Jim said, "Prefer a feast of friends to the giant family."

Illustration: Jesus Christ wearing a crown of thorns and carrying his cross for the sins of mankind. His mother, Saint Mary, approaches him to try to console him as he faced crucifixion.

Photo: The New Rose and New Wine on the
beaches of Grand Haven, Michigan.

In Loving Memory

RANDY R. GODWIN

1958 - 2008

Photo: My late good friend Randy Godwin, an amazing actor and writer, he taught me how to see him and talk to him from the other kingdom. Randy knew I took this flyer of a celebration of his life his service. Randy was a resident artist at the Purple Rose Theatre Company. In Jim's lyrics to "An American Prayer" he mentions, "Resident mockery give us an hour for magic" and "the purple glove"—direct references to the Purple Rose Theatre Company in Chelsea, Michigan, and the amazing art they create.

Photo: The New Rose and the New Wine dancing at a cousin's wedding.

Photo: The New Rose, our adopted son Christopher Joseph,
Saint Mary's next new son, and the New Wine.

Photo: The incredible beauty of our Saint Mary's
Catholic Church in Muskegon, Michigan.

Photo: The amazing bronze statue of Saint Mary outside Saint
Mary's Catholic Church in Muskegon, Michigan. I pray to her with
my right hand covering her clasped bronzed hands of prayer.

Photo: A stunningly beautiful depiction of Son 1 inside Saint Mary's
Catholic Church in Spring Lake, Michigan. This is the "pirate
prince at her side" that Jim also sings about in the song "Wild
Child." The mural is in Saint Mary's Church and across from a
statue of Saint Mary, thus "at her side." Jim could see the future
and son 3 (myself) praying before this image of Son 1 (Jesus) in
the fall of 2016. I believe he did his best to describe the image for
me to pick up where I needed to pray saying the mural resembles
a "pirate prince" because of the blood dripping from the cross.

Photo: A statue of Saint Mary at Saint Mary's Catholic Church in Spring Lake, Michigan. I kneel before her daily to offer prayers for peace, miraculous healing of illnesses, and protection for her new sun. I place my palms above her candles then touch her hands with my warmed hands. She is asking for others to come "petition the Lord with prayer." This particular statue for some reason has the most incredible power, spiritually speaking, that I've ever encountered.

In the Doors song "Wild Child," Jim Morrison directly references his predictive knowledge of him and me praying to this statue of Saint Mary shown above. Consider the lyrics below:

Wild Child

Wild child full of grace
Savior of the human race
Your cool face
Natural child, terrible child
Not your mother's or your father's child
You're our child, screamin' wild
An ancient rulage of grains
And the trees of the night
Ha, ha, ha, ha
With hunger at her heels
Freedom in her eyes
She dances on her knees
Pirate prince at her side
Stirrin' into a hollow idols eyes

There are many references here to my reincarnation with Jim. For instance, he is saying I am a wild child, which I very much was in my teens and twenties. The "full of grace" is the reference to the grace I receive from Saint Mary through sacraments and that I like to think I bestow on others. The "savior of the human race" is also a reference to him and me being sons of Mary and also the conditions in the fall of 2016 with Russia nearly starting a nuclear war around the time of the US presidential election. I sent out an e-mail right before the election showing the photos below and warning of the buildup of ICBMs and ship movements into Syria, which not many Americans were aware of. I'm not sure if my particular e-mail helped sway the election, but I do know that the KGB stated that if Hillary had won, Vladimir Putin was going to start a nuclear war. Jim sings in "Wild Child" that I'm "not your mother's or your father's child, you're our child, screamin' wild," in which he means that while I am born of my natural parents, I am a child of Saint Mary and God the Father just as Jim was too. Jim also mentions "she dances on her knees" and "stirrin' into a hollow idols eyes" these are references to my prayer before this particular statue of Saint Mary. If you were to look at this statue above of Saint Mary in my local town of Spring Lake, Michigan, you would see a hollow look in her eyes of a pale-faced idol or statue. The "dances on her knees" refers to my kneeling in prayer before the statue of Saint Mary.

One other Doors song that references Jim and my souls being merged in the fall of 2016 is the song "Tell All the People." Consider the lyrics below:

Tell All the People

Tell all the people that you see
It's just me
Follow me down
Tell all the people that you see
Set them free
Follow me down

You tell them they don't have to run
We're going to pick up everyone
Come out and take me by my hand
Going to bury all our troubles in the sand, oh yeah
Can't you see the wonder at your feet
Your life's complete
Follow me down

In this song, Jim is basically saying that once our souls were completely merged in the fall of 2016, I should simply tell people I meet in my hometown of Spring Lake and Grand Haven, Michigan, not to worry—that "it's just me," meaning just tell them it's just Jim with me in spirit. Jim also references the healing powers we both will now have through Saint Mary by saying "take us by the hand and we will bury all our troubles in the sand" at the nearby beaches of Grand Haven.

I pray that this very short semi-autobiographical book answers a lot of unanswered questions about both how Jim Morrison left this side of the kingdom and where he is now as well as the return of the Christian kingdom in 2016. The new kingdom is now—I can assure you of that. This is a time of rejoicing. It is not a time of condemnation. It is a time to return to God. I fully realize this doctrine will be scrutinized, debunked, criticized, and possibly condemned. That's precisely why Saint Mary and the Holy Father chose to do it this way. I am only their "new son" and "other jaw," so let's not shoot or crucify the messenger just yet. Mary and I plan to wage a war on war, poverty, greed, injustice, child abuse, racial and gender inequality, human division of any kind, suicide, substance abuse, mental illness, loneliness, and helplessness. Who wants to join us?

I have a list of things to do directly given to me by Saint Mary. I know full well this new dogma may not sit well with official church doctrine. I believe my life on this earth was meant to help fill in the gaps between this side and the other. I'm here to simply help all of us achieve spiritual greatness and defeat the enemy from the darkness. I can assure you the devil exists and is very real. Mother Mary can easily stomp on the snake for you if you let her. This life is all about finding that one person in need, regardless of their circumstances, and going out of your way to lend them a helping hand. It's also about listening to the voice of God and simply doing what he asks you to do in the service of others.

To date I am assisting local authorities with helping to hopefully solve the mystery of what happened to a young lady who was kidnapped and abducted and presumably murdered out here in West Michigan in 2013. While incredibly tragic, the case is quite fascinating, actually, in terms of how spiritual communication can work. A lovely young woman named Jessica Heeringa was kidnapped and murdered in 2013 while working at a local Exxon gas station.

Recently after praying at a Marian statue, I was driving home when I was flashed an image of a koala bear by Jessica's spirit. I stopped by the gas station she was abducted from and asked the attendant if they sold koala bears. He said "No, but the new girl Amanda collects them as a hobby." It was incredible how Jessica was able to provide me with a clue that I could not have guessed had any tie whatsoever to the last place she was seen alive. It also clearly told me that she knew there was a new girl working at the same place she was abducted from and that Jessica knew this girl collected koala bears. I have given many notes to both the lead detective and lead prosecutor in the case.

The other amazing thing that has happened with this case is that this missing girl Jessica also flashed me an image of a wrought-iron *J* with flames covering it. I went online and realized she was referencing the local Double JJ Horse Ranch in nearby Rothbury, Michigan. I asked her sister if the family had ever visited the ranch. Her sister Samantha said they had never been there, but that she had recently taken Jessica's young son to the ranch on a recent trip. It was incredible. Jessica was showing me she could see from the other Kingdom that her son had been on this trip to the Double JJ Horse Ranch with her sister. She also was communicating the Double JJs to mean that "Jessica is now with Jesus." While sadly and tragically this young saint of a woman was taken from this earth, she is now a protective spirit on the branch of lights with Jesus and Saint Mary.

I also had a very profound spiritual experience in assisting a family whose son was recently diagnosed with incurable DIPG brain cancer. DIPG is a cancer in the brain stem near the pons. It is yet to be cured by medical science. I had a former high school football teammate, Jason Carr (son of Hall of Fame coach Lloyd Carr), who had a beautiful son named Chad who tragically passed away from this kind of cancer. It was excruciatingly painful to watch this old friend suffer in this manner. My heart wept for him and his family. The Carr family are a group of amazing people whom I have many great memories with. This other family, the Elkins family from Indiana, is also a wonderful, loving family with three boys. I do not believe children should be suffering from this kind of cancer in this day and age. I can't believe we cannot cure this incurable disease with all the money and technology available to us in this day and age. What is fascinating about this situation is that I would have only encountered their current medical plight by working at my current job. I am a sales representative for an ophthalmology company and call on eye surgeons for a living. One day I was walking in to meet with my physicians and noticed a sign on the check-in desk from the Elkins family of Portage, Indiana. Their son Paxton Elkins, who is seven years old, had recently been diagnosed with DIPG brain cancer. One of my doctors had discovered the tumor after a routine eye exam. The family had placed a flyer on the desk asking for prayers and financial assistance.

I recently had a meeting with the parents where I explained an intuition I had that Saint Mary wanted desperately to help them. In fact, after my friend's son Chad Carr passed away, I could see him actually enter the kingdom of heaven and young Chad flashed me an image of a key that he was holding in his hand. He was asking me to open the gates with Saint Peter with the second key of "Believe." Amazing for only a five-year-old boy to have that kind of knowledge even in the afterlife. On my way driving down to meet with the Elkinses, I stopped at a local Saint Joseph Catholic Church in Saint Joseph, Michigan. While praying in their adoration chapel, I asked Saint Mary to give me some kind of sign that this was what she wanted me to do. Two times I opened the Bible to two separate passages. One was from the book of Malachi that praised the prophet Elijah. The first passage stated that "But for you who fear my name, there will arise the sun of justice with its healing rays." The second passage was from the book of Sirach, and it also extolled Elijah, saying, "By God's word he shut up the heavens and three times brought down fire."

When I consider the meaning of these passages, I think of two of my photos that are enclosed in this book. The first photo shows the sun's healing rays, and the second photo shows what appears to be fire from the earth. When I asked Saint Mary what she wanted me to take away from these passages, she told me to focus on the name meaning of *Elijah*. When I looked up the name Elijah, it translates to "Yahweh is God." Saint Mary then had me look up the last name of the Elkins family, and the name translates directly to the same, "Yahweh is God." I was so completely astounded by the clear message from Saint Mary that I was to assist this family in their struggle. It also was a clear indication Saint Mary had this amazingly brave family in her sights to heal something that science has yet to crack the code to.

We have made plans to pray for young Paxton Elkins at a local Catholic church in front of a statue of Saint Mary and are praying to give this young man Paxton a fighting chance. The name Paxton coincidentally translates to "peace town." I do believe the Prince of Peace himself would like to heal this young man. What is also extremely interesting about this is that Paxton also has a fraternal twin named Landon. This is clearly a sign that ties back into the two "fraternal twin" rainbows that appeared in October of 2016 off the Grand Haven Pier. Jim and I are also Mary's fraternal twins. I have made plans with the family to pray for healing for Paxton on a Monday at Saint Paul's Catholic Church in Valparaiso, Indiana. I was granted special permission to pray for him inside the church, which is coincidentally run by a custodian named— you guessed it—Peter, who just happens to hold all the keys to the church doors too. Monday is a spiritually significant day tied to the new moon of Saint Mary, and coincidentally Paxton is also seven years old.

UPDATE: I met the amazing Elkins family in Valparaiso, Indiana, on Monday, February 6, 2017 at Saint Paul's Catholic Church. Paxton Elkins is so incredible beyond words! He's so full of life and energy, and he's a beautiful child with a beautiful family! We prayed over the "bump" (inoperable brain tumor) in his head to go away. Paxton and his family got to meet Saint Mary at the feet of a wooden statue of her at Saint Paul's, and Paxton asked is this "Mother Earth?" It was so incredible. Today after work I stopped by my local Saint Mary's Church and asked Saint Mary to send the healing Holy Spirit down to Portage, Indiana, where the Elkins family lives and to show me a sign in the sky. It had been snowing all day on Wednesday, February 8, 2017, but I went to the beach at Grand Haven, Michigan, not sure what to expect. On a very overcast and snowy day, all of a sudden, the clouds broke and a small crack of light turned into an image that appeared as a white winged dove (the Holy Spirit) in the sky diving toward the southwest end of the sky. You could see the head and neck and beak of a white bird with its head up and gazing toward the southwest sky, which from Grand Haven points directly toward Portage, Indiana, where the Elkins family lives. It was a clear sign from Saint Mary that the Holy Spirit is diving toward Paxton to help heal him of an incurable, insidious disease that no child should have.

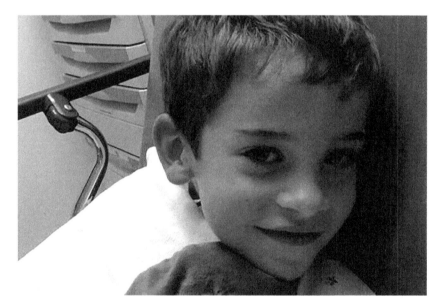

Photo: The amazing, incredibly wonderful Mr. Paxton Elkins, an amazing seven-year-old. Saint Mary has her sights set on his miraculous healing.

Photo: The entire Elkins family of Portage, Indiana. Saint Mary brought me directly to them for healing.

Photo: A white bird of Holy Spirit healing power screaming down from the heavens near Grand Haven, Michigan, toward Portage, Indiana, home of the Elkins family, on Wednesday, February 8, 2017, at approximately 5:00 p.m. EST. The white head of a bird is pointing in the photo down toward the left corner of the frame. You can see a beak on the end of a bird head that is looking up in flight. To the left and right of the diving bird are two wings in flight. This image appeared and was gone within seconds as a cloudy day turned into a breaking sky of light.

As I ponder the incredible white winged dove shown above in this amazing, miraculous photo, I can only think of the lyrics to the "Edge of Seventeen" written and performed by the amazing Stevie Nicks, which was released coincidentally when I was—yes, you guessed it—only seven years old in 1981. Our white winged dove was just in the "nicks of time" one might say. Consider the lyrics from this famous song: "Just like the white, winged dove, sings a song, sounds like she's singing." Within the same minute of the white winged bird of the Holy Spirit appearing off the coast of Grand Haven, Michigan, a powerful 6.3 magnitude earthquake struck off the Coast of Pakistan at approximately 5:03 p.m. EST. This is the exact time the white bird of the Holy Spirit appeared in the skies above Grand Haven, Michigan. When I asked Saint Mary if the earthquake had anything to do with healing for Paxton Elkins, she replied that the literal English translation of Pakistan is "land of the pure." If you pronounce Pakistan, to the ear it sounds phonetically like Paxton. It must be noted there were absolutely no injuries from the Pakistan earthquake; additionally, the earthquake struck off the coast, near the Indian Ocean in—yes, you may have guessed—the Tropic of Cancer.

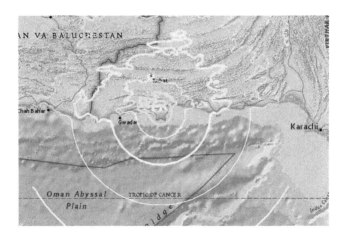

A 6.3 magnitude earthquake hit parts of Balochistan, Pakistan, early on Wednesday morning, the US Geological Survey (USGS) said. It struck at 3:03 a.m. local time, which is 5:03 p.m. EST.

UPDATE: On Thursday, February 9, one day after Saint Mary caused an earthquake in Pakistan for Paxton, she cracked the gates wide open again in Michigan. The new sun appeared in the morning, extremely bright as shown in the photo below. The globe of the sun was shimmering, then it expanded to abnormal size and even became too bright to face. It appeared as a triple sun as well later in the day. Paxton was able to get outside and face the new sun with his new silver cross in hand.

Photo: The new sun appearing brighter and again as a triple sphere in the morning of February 9, 2017, in Michigan. In the Doors song "Not to Touch the Earth" Jim would sing "Sun, sun, sun" to signify this appearance of three suns in one and the three sons of Saint Mary.

Photo: Young Paxton Elkins facing the new sun's healing rays.

Photo: Young Paxton Elkins holding up his white silver cross as he faces the new sun's healing rays. Notice the silver reflection that is bouncing off the cross onto his face. His face is shimmering and glowing in the new sun.

Photo: Paxton Elkins is holding up his new silver cross
toward the new sun on the evening of February 9, 2017, as
the sun shined brightly all day long. The rays are streaking
straight toward Paxton's face through the new cross.

On Thursday, March 23, 2017, I met again with the Elkins'
family at St. Paul's Catholic Church in Valparaiso, Indiana to pray
for more healing for young seven-year-old Paxton Elkins. I had been
praying a lot lately that my book will show the entire world "The Holy
Trinity" through the concept of "infinity." As I prayed with Paxton
who is facing an incredible battle against death, we both placed our
palms together and I asked him if he had anything he wanted to say
to Saint Mary or to Jesus. Without any hesitation Paxton confidently
replied, "yes, please tell them both I love them more than the numbers
that never end." I almost fell over the second I heard him say this.
The implications are quite incredible. A seven-year-old boy who has
probably had very limited formal math education at this point in his
life was demonstrating to me the concept of "mathematical infinity"
which is a very difficult concept for most adults to conceptually
grasp. This amazing seven-year-old was attempting to show the
entire world with this statement that he understood "infinity" as it

relates to science and math as well as our human ability to love and communicate and be one with the spirit world that is for many of us still "unseen." This is quite possibly now the most profound religious experience I have ever had. Please send as many prayers as you can for the entire Elkins family as they battle this "monster" of an insidious disease. I truly believe young Paxton here may be the King we have all been waiting for.

I offer my free services of healing, prayer, clairvoyance, and Catholic insight to anyone who reads this book and wants to receive what I have to offer. I can assure you that with Saint Mary and her three sons on your side, you cannot lose regardless of the circumstances. I am going to leave my personal e-mail and cell phone number right here and now. If you believe in my experiences and you would like to have similar ones, or you simply want special healing, feel free to call or e-mail me or visit me and my family in West Michigan sometime. I can promise you that Saint Mary will show off her new sun to you with its healing rays of justice. If you are a military veteran or a regular citizen and are considering suicide, please, please call me first. My entire reason for being here on this earth in this body and this spirit is simply to help others. I truly believe in every human being's ability to transcend sin and pain and suffering and truly become one together on one branch for all of eternity. May God bless you and bring you to be love for others and to believe in him and his blessed Holy Trinity.

In case you are still on the fence about all of this reincarnation of Jim and Matt via the Catholic Holy Trinity, consider the following undeniable facts. I finished editing this manuscript and submitted it to my publisher (Christian Faith Publishing) on Sunday, February 26, 2017, which is the exact date of Jim's and Matt's combined seventieth birthday. All Jim and I would love to show all of you is how to become infinity through our Holy Trinity. When the ancient Bible prophecies said that Jesus would return, it would be like "a thief in the night." The thief in the night is here to steal your hearts. As Jim once said in his poem "An American Prayer," "All hail the American night." The American night is now a new dawn protected by an American knight who has the authority of three sons of Mary with him. Take full advantage of it, I implore you all. He is here to protect, serve, sacrifice, and lay down his life for you if need be. Jim, Prince Rogers Nelson, and I only want to see you all laughing in the purple rain of my Father's purple reign.

"The snake is long, seven miles, ride the snake, to the ancient lake, he's old and his skin is cold."
"The West is the Best, get here and we'll do the rest."

—Jim Morrison

Sincerely,
Matthew Douglas Pinard and James Douglas Morrison
(734) 649-8431
pinardm@gmail.com

I offer the prayers below for all of us:

Hail Mary

Hail Mary, full of grace.
Our Lord is with you.
Blessed are you among women,
and blessed is the fruit of your womb, Jesus.
Holy Mary, Mother of God,
pray for us sinners,
now and at the hour of our death.
Amen.

Our Father

Our Father who art in heaven
Hallowed be thy name
Thy kingdom has now come
Thy will be done
On earth as it is in heaven
Give us this day our daily bread
And forgive us our trespasses
As we forgive those who trespass
Against us, and lead us not into temptation
But deliver us from evil
For yours is the kingdom, the power, and
The glory, now and forever, amen

About the Author

Matthew Douglas Pinard was born at Saint Joseph Mercy Hospital in 1974 in Ann Arbor, Michigan, three years after Jim Morrison died. Matt was baptized at Saint Mary's Catholic Church in Ann Arbor, Michigan, and attended Detroit Catholic Central High School in Redford, Michigan, where he won a state title in Football in 1990. Matt received his bachelor of psychology degree from the University of Michigan in 1996 and subsequently enlisted in the US Army JAG Corps in the same year. In 2002 Matt graduated with a master's degree in military history from Louisiana State University and then completed a writing apprenticeship at the Purple Rose Theatre Company founded by famed Hollywood actor Jeff Daniels the same year. Matt is a professionally trained theater actor, screenwriter, poet, and this is his first published book. Yes, he can hit every note Jim Morrison ever recorded as well. Matt lives with his wife, Carol Rose, and his adopted son, Christopher Joseph, with their two dogs, Cleetus and Reese, in beautiful Spring Lake, Michigan.

CPSIA information can be obtained
at www.ICGtesting.com
Printed in the USA
FSOW04n0346090617
34830FS